Advanced Praise

"In this simple yet profound book, Valentina shares the secrets of choosing a career path by first learning how to listen to the wisdom of your heart. She then artfully facilitates the reader into taking action in a graceful way, helping to identify and move beyond barriers that may show up. This book is for anyone called to aligning with a vision that is truly a Sacred Yes!"

- **H. Ronald Hulnick, Ph.D.**, president, University of Santa Monica, and **Mary R. Hulnick, Ph.D.**, chief educational officer, University of Santa Monica, coauthors of *Loyalty to Your Soul* and *Remembering the Light Within*

"Get clear on your SACRED YESES! Say YES to what inspires you. Say YES to what you love. Say YES to being more of the real you. Valentina's inspiring new book will help you say YES to living a life you love."

- **Robert Holden Ph.D.**, author of *Authentic Success* and *Happiness NOW!*

T0160307

Get Clear on Your Career

Get
CLEAR
on your
Career

Transformational Lessons to Help You
Find Success and Purpose, and Create a
Life That You Love

VALENTINA SAVELYEVA

NEW YORK

LONDON • NASHVILLE • MELBOURNE • VANCOUVER

Get Clear on Your Career

Transformational Lessons to Help You Find Success and Purpose, and Create a Life That You Love

Published in New York, New York, by Morgan James Publishing in partnership with Difference Press. Morgan James is a trademark of Morgan James, LLC.
www.MorganJamesPublishing.com

ISBN 9781642796391 paperback
ISBN 9781642796407 eBook
ISBN 9781642796414 audio
Library of Congress Control Number:2019950724

Cover Design Concept: Jennifer Stimson

Cover Design: Christopher Kirk www.GFSstudio.com

Interior Design: Chris Treccani www.3dogcreative.net

Editor: Todd Hunter

Book Coaching: The Author Incubator

Morgan James is a proud partner of Habitat for Humanity Peninsula and Greater Williamsburg. Partners in building since 2006.

Get involved today! Visit
MorganJamesPublishing.com/giving-back

For my clients,
whose courage, creativity, and commitment
inspire me daily.

Table of Contents

Introduction

"And the day came when the risk to remain tight in a bud was more painful than the risk it took to blossom."

Meet Roxanne

Roxanne wakes up to the familiar buzzing on her cell. The screen is flashing "6:30 a.m." As she blinks her eyes for a moment, her mind is quiet, still lost in the dream she was having. At thirty-two, she keeps telling herself that she should be able to get away with getting only six hours of sleep at night but it is not working. She feels tired and her double bed feels extra cold this morning. Roxanne has an impulse to turn over and take another five minutes, but she doesn't get a chance. Familiar thoughts enter her mind and assault her peace. She can feel her breath shortening and her head buzzing. "AHHH! Might as well get up!" she thinks. She jumps out and walks into the bathroom, turning on the shower, hoping to tune out the noise in her head, but it's especially loud today.

"I need to figure out my life. I don't know which ideas to pursue. If only I had clarity on what to do, I could move forward and be successful already! There is never enough time to do all that I want. I want to do it all but can't choose. I feel excited by new ideas and projects, but most projects don't go far enough. I am tired of juggling part-time gigs to get my business off the ground. Maybe I should have kept my marketing job before I had more clarity on what to do next. I just want my career to make sense and I want my life and me to make sense!"

"I still l have some money left over even though I quit a year ago. I guess that is good. But I am so tired of having inconsistent cash inflow from part-time projects with start-ups! I am avoiding looking at the bank statements, as I know my savings are running low. I don't understand why I can't generate money with all the ideas that I have! I have two graduate degrees, and I was voted one of the most likely people to succeed in high school, so why am I still here at thirty-two?!"

"I can't understand how I can be so 'gifted' (so everyone is telling me) and feel not good enough. I feel like I am wasting my life! Where is my big life? I feel so impotent with all the big ideas and big visions that keep coming to me. So frustrating! When will I ever feel good enough to do it? When will I have clarity about my life and my career path?"

"I feel like I have failed everyone. I am not making the difference that I know I can make. I hate this feeling of not being able to take care of others and myself. I am beginning to feel really tied down and constricted because I need to make money, and I am pissed that I may need to go back to marketing and give up the idea of doing what I love and believe in!"

"I am feeling overwhelmed and tired most of the time. Mom says I need to get married, I probably should. Look at my life! What have I really accomplished?"

"I know I need to pick a direction for my career, and if that is growing my business, I need to make it profitable. I need to make a bigger difference in this world. I need to express my truth. I feel like a fraud, like I am hiding the truth of who I am. I need more time to follow up and manifest the ideas that I have. I want to be much further along! I am so afraid of dying with regret, and yet regret is here already. My biggest fear is that I will die feeling that life was not worth living, that I didn't get to 'sing my song.' And yet, days are slipping by. And what have I done? NOTHING!"

Roxanne's thoughts get interrupted by a loud beeping from her iPhone on the bathroom sink. She reluctantly stumbles out of the steaming shower, grabs the towel to dry her fingers and presses the red stop button on the blinking screen. It is 7:00 a.m. and Roxanne is already exhausted and is tempted to crawl back to bed and fall sleep.

This is a regular morning for Roxanne, that is until she becomes fed up and takes a stand. She starts looking for support and gets a referral to my coaching practice.

When Roxanne shows up in my virtual office on Zoom, she claims to be desperate for support for getting clarity with how to proceed. She can't understand why she has been having so much trouble with moving forward.

Roxanne is a beautiful woman, incredibly smart and creative and easily connects with others. It is not unlike her to meet someone in line at Peet's Coffee and then be offered a job interview by the time she has ordered her latte. Her work in marketing used to be highly recognized, and in her twenties, she was promoted quickly during the five years that she was working in the corporate world. But she had to leave. It just didn't feel true to what her heart wanted. She felt stifled. She felt like a fraud. She needed to get out.

There are so many inspirational stories about people starting businesses or creating positions that are unique and make such a positive impact. This is what excites Roxanne. She knows that she wants to be one of these successes. So she takes a romantic plunge and quits her marketing job without any clear plans for what is next. She is flying high for a few months, but now a year and a half later, she is feeling flat and dull. So many projects haven't gone very far, and she is not even sure if she still wants to grow her business, do consulting, get a full-time job in marketing, or do something completely different.

Hidden Epidemic of Lack of Clarity

Roxanne is not alone and there are so many of us, who find ourselves in situations that were unexpected. How can we have so much potential and recognition early on and then feel so stuck and confused later? What is wrong with this picture? It seems that the only people who don't have this problem are the ones who are either very fortunate and pick the right path off the bat or the ones who choose not to rock the boat and not ask the uncomfortable questions – such as "What is it that I really, really want to do?" And, "Why am I still here not doing that? How can I move forward?"

For Roxanne it seems that her personal life has been feeling stuck and dull too. She can't decide on a life partner either because she can't decide on what kind of work and life she wants to have. Even though she enjoys the attention, her dating life isn't really unfolding the way she thought it would be by this stage.

Get Clear on Your Career is my love letter to Roxanne and to everyone else who has the courage and willingness to discover what it is they are called to contribute to this world and how to move forward. This book is for those who are ready to let go of the training wheels and to test out what they can do. This book is for those who are ready to face their messy questions, fears, and feelings and begin finding answers.

This book is for dreamers who are ready to move past the "wishing phase" into "I am taking steps and creating a life that I actually want to live" phase. This is the book for those who are ready to grow up, but not in a "settling down" kind of way. It is for those who are ready to define for themselves what growing up means. This book is a guide for those who are ready to create the career and life that is deeply aligned with all parts of them.

Chapter 1:

My Path to Clarity

"Happiness is not something ready made.
It comes from your own actions."
— DALAI LAMA

Journey of Hunger

Come with me to Russia. The year is 1989. It is early March in a small-town square, surrounded by identical gray boxy buildings, piles of melting snow are all around. A line of people is stretching out in an S shape, mostly old *babushkas* covered in thick gray shawls and school kids. A skinny eight-year-old girl with frizzy blond hair wearing a bright-red coat that is two sizes too small is fidgeting in line. That eight-year-old girl is me. A woman with thick blue eye shadow who smells like

1

cigarettes comes over and grabs my wrist. She scribbles the number 134 with a blue ink and moves on. That is my number in line for today. I look up across the square to read the sign "Grocery Store." My stomach growls. I hope they will have enough bread and butter by the time I make it to the entrance.

I close my eyes, and for a moment, I go to my familiar fantasy world – where I often escape. There is a table there that is covered in white cloth and on top is filled with food, all kinds of breads, roasted chicken, butter, milk, and, of course, lots of pastries. I imagine myself and my six-year-old sister eating so much we cannot take another bite, and there is still so much food that is left. I smile with imaginary bliss as I feel an impatient tap in between my shoulder blades. I am back at the square with the melting snow. I notice that a gray figure in front of me has moved forward, so I take the next step.

Since I was very young, I was driven by hunger. The physical hunger later translated into the hunger for learning all kinds of subjects and collecting experiences. I didn't think much about it, and it has allowed me to achieve what most considered a high level of success. But inside I was always hungry for more, and I refused to choose or settle for one of anything. No matter how much I enjoyed something or someone inevitably I would want more of something or someone else.

It was fun at school. I remember at UC Berkeley I loved that I could study finance in the morning, do ballet in the afternoon, and teach a course in women's leadership in the evening. I had it all – Dean's List with a 3.98 GPA, full time offer at a major investment bank with a sweet signing bonus, dance performances, a boyfriend who adored me, lots of very interesting friends from all over the planet, and dreams to change the world by the age of thirty.

Then I graduated. And life began to push back. As much as I was stimulated and challenged by my job in investment banking, I quickly began to feel stifled and wanted something more meaningful and liberating and I was craving a way to express my gifts as a performing artist. So once I have completed my two-year program as an analyst, I collected my bonus and moved to New York City to attend one of the most prestigious professional dance programs in the United States while also auditioning and dancing around the city.

I dove into the dance scene in New York, and for several years, I thrived living the life that I had dreamed about since I took my first ballet class at age seven back in Russia. I loved the new "home" that I found in the sunny, airy newly-built dance studio a few blocks away from the Broadway with the floor-to-ceiling mirrors and the long wooden ballet barres. I felt a sense of purpose and belonging as I showed up with a discipline that I had learned in my years as an investment banker to work on my ballet, jazz and modern dance technique for five hours a day. And then I enjoyed a more relaxed vibe in the dingier older studios in downtown New York City, where I often rehearsed on the projects that I was involved in. I was taking in as much as I could – the drama of the auditions, seeing dance and theatre productions on the best stages of the city, running around in the pink ballet tights, and even the crying spurts to pick myself back up from the never-ending physical pain in my body as much as from the emotional pain as I was being picked apart and criticized every single day along with all the other dancers. I loved and welcomed it all, but I also quickly began to feel unbalanced and unfulfilled, so I greatly appreciated my part-time gig of assisting instructors with MBA-level finance courses on the weekends.

As the years went on, I was getting more and more burned out by my dance career, which was not unfolding as fast or as big as I had expected, and I eagerly shifted into teaching finance courses full time, which was a lot more fun for me. Once again, I thrived and I was sure this was it! I was flying weekly all over the United States and Europe. I was teaching at the top MBA programs and financial firms, getting inspired daily by my students, who were brilliant, creative and hungry for life and for learning. I was receiving raving reviews both from the students and from my team. And yet, as I was growing as a finance trainer, being invited to teach at larger and more advanced audiences, I could hear that whisper once again that said, "This is not it; do not commit."

This time I didn't want to listen and I let myself enjoy teaching for a while, while at the same time receiving my MA in spiritual psychology from the University of Santa Monica. I figured taking psychology classes would balance me out, and it did for a short amount of time. And yet, I would have moments when I would imagine myself doing work similar to what my favorite authors and coaches were doing, leading workshops, publishing books and supporting people with finding work and creating lives that they loved. These visions and inner nudges always felt bitter sweet. Eventually, the inner voice became louder and louder and finally after almost ten years with the training company, I announced my decision to leave my teaching family and dove into the coaching, writing and speaking on the subjects of success and personal transformation.

What I didn't realize at the time, but soon became very aware of once I quit, was how much more was tied into my unwillingness to commit to a career. On the outside, I thought my major problem was that I had too many talents and interests and that I didn't know how to choose and that it was relatively harmless to wait until I was ready. However, once I stopped running and distracting myself, I saw how heavy the price tag was for my earlier indecision.

The Real Price of Indecision

One area of my life where I was paying a very high price for my indecision around my career was my romantic partnership. Even though I had been with my partner for eleven years at the time, I was still refusing to get married because subconsciously I couldn't see a future with anyone since I couldn't see a future for myself and my work. I am realizing now how much time I have wasted on trying to solve the problem of not being willing to commit in my relationship. The truth was that I didn't know how to trust myself with making big decisions, so, of course, it showed up in my personal life. Interestingly enough, as soon as I started to apply the tools that I will share in this book and got clear on what to do, I also became clear on wanting to move on from the relationship, which was very challenging and yet necessary for me to do in order to step into the life that I have now.

Another area where I was paying a high price for my indecision around the career were my finances. To be honest, I thought I was doing amazing. I was earning over $250,000 a year, not including my partner's salary. We were living in a luxurious apartment on the twenty-fifth floor in midtown Manhattan with floor-to-ceiling windows and a view that was equally captivating during the day and the night. We were dining at great restaurants almost daily, staying at fun hotels all over the United States and Europe for my work and for fun, and I was enjoying the freedom to travel, to take any self-development classes that I wanted, to support charities, and to attend my beloved Broadway musicals and plays. However, when I slowed down after I quit, I also began to see how much money I had wasted over the years on things that I didn't really want. I was doing so to simply numb the subtle feelings of being unsatisfied or to numb the voice whispering to me to explore doing something more meaningful with my life and my relationship. I also became painfully aware of the many investing opportunities that I had missed, not because of lack of know-how or skill, but because I was too busy keeping myself distracted from the discomfort of listening to the inner voice that kept telling me that I was meant to do something else.

During the last few years as a corporate finance instructor, even though I was very highly regarded by both students and colleagues, I noticed that I often felt slightly jealous of those who were being bold and courageous, who were taking risks with their lives. I remember I would watch many inspirational speakers and coaches give talks on YouTube, and as motivated as I would be, I would feel jealous that they dared to live the life that deep down I wanted. I would talk myself out of doing what they were doing by reminding me that I was loving my life. Add to that, I supported thousands of students every year and I loved everyone I worked with. My team had nurtured me for almost ten years, and I considered them to be my family. So here I was, with a job that I genuinely enjoyed, with lots of love and support, with a ring on my finger from the partner who adored me. And yet, toward the end, I started to wake up anxious in the middle of the night and kept going on Netflix binges to numb out the nagging feeling that this is not the life that I wanted.

I thought my problem was to get clear and choose what to do with my career, but it turned out to be a lot more than that. It was about choosing what kind of life I wanted to live. And as glamorous and exciting as my life looked, I began to feel like an imposter. It was a perfect life, the only thing – or, to be more precise, the only person – that didn't "fit" was me.

As the inner intensity built, I knew that I had to quit and to temporarily be very uncomfortable as I dove into the unknown.

Turn Around

Thankfully, parallel to the journey I just described, I was also deeply involved in the area of self-development, reading hundreds of books, attending conferences on leadership and transformation, and studying with teachers and coaches since before I was twenty. As I was finishing up my time teaching finance, I began to use the tools that I will be sharing in this book that I have since very successfully used with many of my clients who were going through a career shift.

The turning point in my own journey came when I mastered some of the big keys – learning how to make choices and take action from a place of inner connection to my deeper wisdom, learning how to work with myself so that I could make commitments that I actually kept, and learning how to work with fears and doubts that inevitably showed up.

My own career shift was not an easy one. The transition process stripped me raw of any old identifications of who I thought I was. Tearfully, I said goodbye to my beloved students and the training team, and to the airy twenty-fifth floor apartment in midtown New York City, as I opened my private coaching practice and moved to a second-floor apartment on a quiet block in Venice, CA. Shortly after I said goodbye to my best friend and my life partner of eleven years, dropped off about 90 percent of my possessions at a local Goodwill store and moved again to my new home in Santa Monica, CA. Over the course of a year and a half, I let go of all the major "roles" that I used to identify myself by and now I was facing a completely new life.

Say Yes to a New Life

Life responded with new clients whom I loved, new deeper friendships and partnerships, an improved relationship with myself, better health, stronger finances and a general expansion in all areas of my life.

I am writing this chapter in my Santa Monica apartment, with a light breeze coming through the open balcony door as I watch the leaves on the trees gently blowing in the warm wind. I just walked in from a walk on the beach with a close friend and responded to some emails from the clients. Later this afternoon I will take a yoga class, check in on my clients in the coaching group on Facebook, and speak to a couple of referrals who are interested in the program, before I meet with a friend for dinner. My life feels graceful. It is not easy, as I am continuously stretching myself with new challenges – publishing this book is certainly a long-held dream for me. I am growing as I am facing these challenges, and yet, not a single day goes by that I don't feel a sense of purpose, knowing that the life that I am living with all its beauty, love, prosperity, joy, messiness, and sweetness, is mine. My life feels so aligned with all parts of me that I feel truly at home in it for the first time.

That is my wish for you in this book: to help you avoid the challenges of my own journey by sharing what I have learned, and to support you to find the work that you love and build a life where you feel at home.

Chapter 2:

The CLEAR WAY Framework

"It takes courage to grow up and
turn out to be who you really are."
— E.E. CUMMINGS

How to Use This Book

This book is meant to be a guide for the process of gaining clarity around what you want to do, around how you make choices, and around how you want to proceed. I am sharing the tools and practices that I have been using with my clients and in my own personal life. Some of these tools will resonate more than others. Some of these practices may bring forward discomfort, just as I experienced when I started to metaphorically "defog my glasses" and began to see that there is a lot more that I had been unwilling to see besides choosing what to do.

The next eight chapters cover eight keys in various areas that cumulatively will support you in not only getting clear regarding what you want to do, but also in moving forward, and in taking action steps in a successful way.

At the end of each chapter, I will share some suggested exercises that you could practice with, if you choose. You are welcome to dive in as much or as little as you like. In my experience, the value of any idea is in its application and in many ways you won't know if something works unless you try it wholeheartedly.

If you are ready to dive in, you can either read the book cover to cover and then go back and do the exercises that stand out for you. Or you can take one key area at a time and work with it before moving forward. You can work through them in the order that I have them or you can go back and forth. In many ways, each one is meant to support the other, so I invite you to trust your instincts on how to digest the information. You may want to read this book with a friend to dive in deeper together.

However you choose to do it, I invite you to have fun with the process and give yourself permission to be open, messy, and curious about what may be available for you. One of my friends and a fellow coach often says that "we don't know what we don't know." I love that. I invite you to get curious about *you*.

* * *

The CLEAR WAY Framework to Find Professional Success

C: Cultivate a State Where Clarity Is Possible

In Chapter 3, you will have an opportunity to begin working with the tools for how to tap into a clarity state in a very intentional and practical way. You will also learn how to distinguish the need for clarity of the bigger vision for your career versus the need for clarity of the next steps. And finally, you will be introduced to various tools for accessing your inner wisdom as you begin to develop practices for how to discern making choices that feel aligned and genuinely true for you.

L: Learn How to Dream Effectively

In Chapter 4, you will explore your relationship with dreaming and setting goals. In my experience, most people who come into my practice have a disconnect in this area and most people don't allow themselves to truly embrace wanting and put caps on dreams. You will learn tools for removing any self-imposed caps and limitations, so as you choose your niche and your next steps, you will never have to "settle" ever again.

E: Enlist a Vision That Is a Sacred YES!

In Chapter 5, you will be invited to go even deeper into connecting to your heartfelt desires and dreams and to explore what may be underneath your wants and dreams. You will have an opportunity to identify what it is that you really, *really* want. I will introduce tools for "trying out dreams for size" before "buying" and investing years into them, and you will have an opportunity to enroll your Future Self to assist you in choosing your path today. Finally, you will learn practices for easily identifying next steps and to begin building the momentum for action.

A: Access Your Personal Success Formula

In Chapter 6, you will learn tools and practices for identifying your own formula for success that has already been proven to work for you. I will share coaching tips on the art of making and keeping agreements and you will get a chance to apply both your personal success formula and your personal way of making commitments to assist you with choosing what to do and moving into action.

R: Receive Maximum Return on Your Energy Investments

In Chapter 7, you will get more intimate with how you currently manage your energy. I will share some unexpected ways that energy often leaks and the tools for how to cultivate and nourish the natural energy cycles for maximum success. You will identify and incorporate routines and practices that will allow you to use your energy in the most effective way as you continue to move forward toward your Sacred YES vision.

W: Wire Resistance to Work for You

In Chapter 8, I will talk about the reason why resistance shows up and how to work with it to not only prevent it from stopping you from moving forward but to also accelerate your progress. If you read only one chapter, I suggest reading this one. Or if you notice yourself resisting exercises, even if you like the concepts, this is a good chapter to read for the extra tips and context for how to work with the resistance. My intention here is to show how to "employ" your resistance to work *for* you instead of allowing it to destroy any progress you make, which is the default for most of my incoming clients.

A: Align Thoughts and Emotions for Success

In Chapter 9, I will invite you to go deeper into the arena of the inner work and explore the tools and practices for removing doubts and fears that will inevitably show up. This is another chapter that you might want to reference often at every stage of your process of choosing what to do and as you move into the action.

Y: Yield Financial Results That You Desire

Finally, your journey of choosing what to do would be incomplete if I did not address the elephant in the room – the money. So, in Chapter 10, I will introduce the tools for identifying any blind spots around money and financial prosperity. Some of these blind spots may come as a surprise to you. And yet, most likely, they have been holding you back from bringing the income, or keeping and enjoying the income that you were able to generate in the past. I will support you in identifying and removing any stigma and fears around being able to talk about money in a healthy confident way, which will be necessary for the interviews, salary negotiations, fundraising, hiring, and any other money-related tasks that your new career may require. And as a bonus, I will introduce some tools and practices that many of my clients have used to cultivate a healthy, long-term partnership with money in their lives that will support you not only in shifting into the career that you love but also in creating a life of long-term, sustainable financial success that you enjoy.

* * *

It is my wish for you that by the end of reading this book, you will see not only that it is possible for you to choose what to do professionally from a place of deep alignment, authenticity, and joy but also that making choices from the place of the inner clarity and alignment is, in my experience, the easiest and most effortless way to shift into the work and life that's destined for you.

I love this quote by George Eliot: "It is never too late to be what you might have been."

So, as you dive into the stories and the exercises, I invite you to get very curious about you, and set the intention to be open, receptive, and willing to test out for yourself what works and what doesn't work for you. And above all else, I invite you to have fun with the process!

Chapter 3:

Cultivate a State
Where Clarity Is Possible

"Finding requires giving up the game of seeking."
— Shanti Christo Foundation, Way of Mastery

Hidden Truth about Clarity

Most people who come into my practice mention that they want to experience more clarity in their lives and share how much they focus on trying to figure things out in hopes that once they do, they will be able to move forward with their jobs, businesses, relationships, and life in general. I hear a lot of complaining about being stuck, sometimes for months and sometimes for years. And of course, getting clear on what to do becomes a key goal and a key challenge to reach. So most new clients share how they have been working hard on "getting clarity", usually by doing more research, by taking more career placement tests, by scanning through the job postings or some other activity that requires more doing. And as valuable as all of these activities are they typically are not enough for the person to get clear and move forward.

Here is what I discovered after the two decades of personal growth work and thousands of hours of conversations with both the MBA students and later the coaching clients - the process of "getting to clarity" is really a misnomer. I claim that clarity is better described as a state of *awareness* or a state of *being* and is not an automatic byproduct of some complicated thinking exercise, or gathering research, or a similar type of activity. Better yet, I want to show you how reaching and residing in a state of clarity is a skill that can be cultivated. This skill can be mastered by everyone and will make all the other activities (such as doing research) a lot more effective.

Let me explain.

Most of my clients (and I certainly can relate) have been trained to think that if they have more information they can do a comprehensive analysis (preferably with a list of pros and cons) that will help them get clear and have an answer to whatever question or a problem they face.

I am not an exception. This is a bit embarrassing to admit, but I once evaluated a marriage proposal by creating a list of pros and cons before I said yes.

I still remember that proposal. I was standing on a wobbly wooden deck, feeling the warm ocean breeze, trying to keep my balance. It was my partner's and my first night on the magical island of Vieques, Puerto Rico. The sun was setting and strips of pink were spreading across the blue sky. My best friend of five years was on one knee holding a sparkling diamond ring waiting for my answer. I was gulping for air, frozen with indecision. Finally, after what felt like an eternity I sheepishly requested to think about it. I spent the rest of the trip and the following week creating a pros and cons list on my iPhone for whether I should say yes or no. The pros list far outweighed the cons, and I finally said yes. In my innocence, I was expecting everything else to flow effortlessly from then on. But, as you can imagine, it didn't. Five years later, I was still dragging my feet, finding excuses why I couldn't commit to a date and plan a wedding. Eventually, I returned the ring and left the relationship.

My story of relying on the logical process for making decisions may be extreme, but in my experience, most people secretly hope that there is a way to "outsource" their choices and decision-making to some external process, preferably a very logical one, or they let another person or a test make a decision for them. I have learned firsthand that, sooner or later, life catches up and poses the same question again and again, and it did so until I was willing to answer with my heart and my mind.

You may not be as deep in the weeds in your decision-making process as I used to be, but a part of you may still believe that if you don't have clarity you need more information. Sometimes that is accurate. For example, if you are buying a new phone or a new computer, you understandably will need some information to make a decision. But here is the catch, at a certain point the information will become overwhelming and harmful, due to its size, the mind will not be able to process it all, as it is trying to logically evaluate (the left part of our brain) all the factors and unless it is a very "black-and-white" situation, the mind often begins going in circles, as it gets stuck in the "gray area" of emotions, social influences, and similar.

Information gathering is important; however, it is only one of the steps. And most people stop there. The next step that will actually support you in assimilating the information so that you can digest it and make a decision involves the right part of the brain and the heart. This is the stage when you want the mind chatter to get quiet so that you can connect to what is important to you. This is the part that most people that I see coming into my practice struggle with. And this is the part that is crucial to experiencing clarity.

Connect to the State of Inner Clarity

One of the first exercises I do with the clients who are looking for clarity is inviting them to recall an event or an experience when they made a decision that they were very clear on, when there was no shadow of a doubt in their mind. Everyone has a decision like this to recall. And when I inquire deeper, the clients usually share that when their mind was quiet, the decision looked very simple and felt good in their body. Even if there was a lot to do, there was no drama around the decision. I hear terms like *calm focus, peaceful, warm, expansive, no mind chatter*. Everyone describes it as a state of *being*.

My intention in this chapter is to share some tools and practices with you to support you in cultivating this state of clarity, so that you can begin to apply it to all decisions on your journey of choosing what to do.

Clarity of the Entire Vision Versus Clarity of the Next Steps

Before I jump into the tools for cultivating clarity, I want to bring up another important distinction that most of my clients who are highly successful integrate early on. Most clients who come in confused are innocently waiting for the clarity of the entire vision of their career – be that a business or a job role – so as a result they wait, and wait, and wait, and continue feeling stuck and unable to move forward.

Here is a little secret that I discovered that is a key distinction between those clients who stay stuck and those who begin to move forward quickly. The clients who say stuck tend to wait until they have clarity about the entire vision for their new career, while the clients who begin to move forward quickly focus on cultivating clarity for the next steps and lean into action. Yes, it is amazing to receive a download from "the Universe" for the entire vision for a new career or a new business; however, most of my clients (and I am certainly in this category) do not experience clarity that way. And that is great! Because they are not limiting themselves by the full picture of the vision that they "downloaded." What I learned is that when the clients yearn for clarity, what they really want to know is what to do next, which direction to choose to lean into. And that is usually a lot more accessible and much easier to get an answer to. And there are so many great things about that.

One thing is that the "price tag" that the client pays for each action step is very small, which helps with the flexibility to adapt. Since the client is not waiting for all the details of the entire vision, once she gets clear on the direction and picks an action step, she moves forward. Then, if a particular action step doesn't work out right away, she is not as emotionally attached to that action as she would have been if she had spent years on working out the entire vision, so she can typically adjust more easily by taking a modified action step. As a result, she keeps moving forward instead of getting stuck and needing to go back to the drawing board every time she hits a roadblock.

Another great benefit, and I see this every time I work with a client, is that no matter how big the client's vision is, once she begins to lean into it, as she grows, her vision grows with her. So why would I want to limit myself by requesting clarity up-front and then keeping myself in a box that I created? It is like requesting that a five-year-old chooses his profession or a décor for his room and then expect him to live there and enjoy his choices as an adult. It may work out, but most likely as the person grows, so do his choices for the décor and the career.

So I invite you to set the intention to experience states of clarity and focus on the next steps, to choose a direction to lean into, and to allow the vision to unfold, knowing that as you grow, the vision will grow too.

With this intention in mind, let's dive deeper into the tools for cultivating states of clarity.

Uncover the "Benefits" of Staying Confused

I had a client, Natasha. She was in her late thirties and multitalented on many levels. She had a successful decade in corporate America under her belt before she opened a business focusing on bringing wellness practices to companies. She had an abundance of ideas and easily connected with potential clients. However, she struggled making the ends meet and found herself overwhelmed by the sheer number of ideas and paths that she could take as she kept switching from focusing on one client to another, never fully closing any deals, and most of her brilliant ideas were not taking off. When she came into my practice, she stated that she was committed to figuring out, once and for all, what she wanted to do. However, when we started digging deeper, I probed her with a few questions, such as if there were any benefits, maybe hidden ones, from her state of staying "confused"? She went quiet, and then she started to cry as she realized how the confusion in her life kept her "safe" by convincing her to play small and prevented her from taking bold action and taking any risks. She began to see that she was more invested in staying "safe" in her confusion than she was committed to solving her problems and moving forward. This was a painful realization for Natasha, and she gave herself space to work with all the feelings of regret and judgments of having wasted precious time. She saw how much it cost her in terms of energy and lost opportunities. However, as she went deeper, she let go of her attachment to searching and allowed herself to connect to the state of the quiet focus. I call it the state of "inner clarity" that is always there. And things began coming into focus for her.

Like with Natasha, one of the first tools that I share with my clients is to identify and address any hidden benefits and attachments they may have to staying confused.

Clarity Is Found in a Quiet Mind

Most of you probably didn't expect a book on choosing which professional path to pursue to talk about mindfulness; however, with all the years of working with so many professionals at various stages of choosing careers, I came to see again and again that those who were able to cultivate a practice of calming their mind so that they could connect to the state of inner clarity – where all the information that accumulated could be used most effectively – were the most successful.

So what tools can you use to cultivate a quieter mind? There are countless possibilities and some of you may already have some of these practices as a part of your life. If not, I highly recommend experimenting with one or two to incorporate something that works and supports you especially through this process of choosing what to do next in your career.

The following are some practices that my clients have used to cultivate the state of a quiet mind that might work for you:

- Meditation
- Prayer
- Walking
- Hiking
- Singing / chanting
- Mindful breathing

- Counting objects of certain color (I had a client who loved doing that)
- Boxing
- Weight lifting/doing very physical workouts
- Swimming
- Yoga
- Making art
- Watching birds / wild life

As you can see the list is endless. However, it is not the activity but the intention of how you engage in the activity that matters. The clients who were the most successful would show up with the intention of experiencing a state of mindfulness, being fully present here and now, and experiencing a state of a calm focus.

The mind is a like a muscle. If you want to develop strength, you can't plan to go to the gym once or twice and then expect to be competing in Olympics. You want to develop a practice for training the mind to stay in a state of being fully present and focused.

If you love science, the intention for this exercise is to engage the right hemisphere of the brain as well as to create a more "balanced" brain activity in general as the brain waves go from an anxiety producing high Beta wave state to a more grounded and productive low Beta mixed with Alpha waves or even deeper.

Most of my clients, especially those who do a lot of "thinking" and "logical" type of work, are trained to engage the left hemisphere of the brain, and they are very, very good at it. However, that part of the brain is designed to process concepts in a very linear fashion and cannot comprehend or experience the state of being present, here and now. It is simply not wired for that.

The right hemisphere on the other hand, is the part that gets activated during artistic activities and is the part that is nonlinear and where a person can have experiences of knowing in an instant.

My invitation for all of you is to become a more balanced human being and to cultivate the mastery of both. The goal here is that as you collect all the information to evaluate your career choices, you have the mind "muscles" to digest the options and make a decision from a place of confidence.

Meet Your Inner Coach

Once a client begins practicing mindfulness, I make an invitation to connect with and hire the inner coach (often referred to as the intuition, the gut feeling, or the inner wisdom) as a guide on this journey.

For some of you, intuition is a big part of how you make decisions. However, most clients that struggle with clarity have been taught to value the logical mind more. My intention here is to expand your tools for making decisions.

Imagine that you are your own company. You are the CEO, and you have lots of employees. Imagine you are having a board meeting and someone is speaking. That is the voice that is loud in your head right now. Curious about which voice it is?

When I take clients through this exercise, most of them notice that the predominant voice in their head that is "running the meeting" is the voice of a critic. I ask them to name that character, and I have heard so many fun names. However, the characteristics are pretty devastating: critical, harsh, judgmental, requires complete perfection, is never satisfied, shuts down all creative impulses. When I go deeper with the clients, the inner critic often reminds them of someone critical in their lives early on – a parent, a teacher, or a blend of a few key people. Well, what kind of a meeting result do you think you will have if you continue letting the inner critic run it? Forget clarity about choosing what to do, you are lucky if you can make it through an hour without wanting to call it quits and just turn on Netflix.

Attacking the inner critic will not do you any good and will only give the inner critic more power, as it loves combat. Instead, engage another "employee" – the one who nudged you to pick up this book, the one who nudged you to make some of the earlier decisions in your life where you experienced clarity, the one who keeps whispering in your ear that you are meant for something more, that the secret dreams and aspirations you had as a kid or a teenager actually were seeds for something. That voice. I refer to it as the inner coach. You can call it anything you like. I would begin to get to know your inner coach and begin to give it the speaking slot at the meeting in your head. Get to know how he/she speaks to you. Do you get a feeling in your gut? Do you have a temperature change? Do you experience its voice as a calm wisdom or a remembrance of something that you already knew? Keep getting to know your inner coach and keep inviting him or her to run the meetings and, hopefully, eventually your entire company.

I personally have experienced many shifts in my life, especially over the past three years, and I could not have made any of these decisions if I hadn't dedicated years to cultivating my relationship with my inner coach. Now I cannot imagine making any decisions without her guidance. It is so simple; it is like having the wisest and kindest mentor on call 24/7, free and always available.

I invite you to begin incorporating some of the practices for quieting the mind, identifying and working through any blind spots around secret/hidden benefits of staying confused, and hiring your inner coach to run this project of choosing the next steps in your career.

Chapter Highlights

- Clarity is a state of awareness that you can cultivate.
- Setting the intention to experience clarity of the next steps is much more effective and action producing than waiting to experience clarity of the entire career, which may be limiting and too rigid to take action from.
- Incorporating practices that activate the right hemisphere of the brain and facilitate quieting the mind chatter is a first step in cultivating a state of clarity.

- Identifying and dissolving blind spots around any attachment to staying confused is another important tool in becoming more clear.
- Hiring your inner coach to be the project lead on this journey of choosing your career is a fun and a very powerful way to proceed.

Suggested Exercises and Next Steps

- Incorporate a mindfulness practice into your daily life. Test out a few to find one that fits you and your life.
- Go through the exercise of self-inquiry. What are the hidden benefits of staying confused? What is the cost? What would you need to let go of to move forward? Whom would you need to upset or disappoint to move forward? What inner and outer choices are you making that perpetuate the state of staying confused? What alternative choices could you make that could lead to a different result?
- Name your inner critic and your inner coach. Spend some time with both, but especially your inner coach. What is she/he like? How do you best connect with them? Remind yourself throughout the day to give the speaking floor to your inner coach. You can begin practicing with small daily decisions, like consult your inner coach when you are choosing what to eat for lunch or which movie to watch and then expand to bigger decisions.

* * *

In the next chapter, I will take the conversation deeper into removing any hidden caps you may have put on yourself as it relates to dreaming and wanting.

Chapter 4:

Learn How to Dream Effectively

"The greater danger for most of us lies not in setting our aim too high and falling short; but in setting our aim too low, and achieving our mark."
— MICHELANGELO

"We can never have enough of what we didn't want in the first place."
— ROBERT HOLDEN, *AUTHENTIC SUCCESS*

Re-Learn How to Dream

Once my clients have a hold on cultivating the states of clarity, I invite them to explore their relationship with wanting and dreaming. Together we slow down and examine very carefully to discover any blind spots around what they say they want or don't want. What I've learned is that the clients who tend to move forward and create an incredible level of success are the ones who also are not afraid to dream big, in a way that lights them up.

My intention is to dive deeper and share the tools for cultivating the skill of healthy and productive wanting and dreaming (or reclaiming something that we all did naturally as kids) in a way that will be the most supportive with not only choosing your career but also with the moving forward and staying focused and motivated.

Dreams Powered by Fear Versus Dreams Powered by Love

Many clients come in and claim that they want to make a bigger difference with their work, or to make more money, or to get married and have a balanced and full life. Even though the dreams may sound similar, I notice two very distinct ways that these goals and dreams could be powered. One source is love and the other is fear.

Let me share the story of Alexis. A few years ago, I began working with Alexis, a hardworking and stylish professional in her mid-thirties who was living a fast paced life in Chicago. Alexis hired me because she wanted to make sure she didn't get fired from her job – again. Alexis had been fired from two other jobs and was very nervous. Her desire was understandable and it was clear it was coming from fear. At that point, Alexis was so focused on keeping her job, she couldn't even imagine being happy doing something that she loved. As we began working together and healing Alexis's fears and hidden limitations around dreaming, she began to relax and about five months into our work together, Alexis came into a session with an announcement: she had always had a heartfelt dream as a kid and young adult to start her own business. But then she buried it; she hadn't thought of it in a decade, but now she was ready to dive in. This new dream of starting a business had brought up its own list of fears and insecurities, through which we worked, but it was rooted in a very different place. It was rooted in Alexis's heart. I was not surprised that Alexis connected to it at this time, as she was allowing herself more space to connect to her heart and had more confidence and trust in herself by then. Needless to say, Alexis got two other partners and opened her company within a year.

Dreams powered by fear can take us to a certain level. For example, I have seen many clients being motivated by fear of needing to pay their bills to get creative in their business or being motivated by fear and preparing for an interview to get a new job. However, fear can only take you up to a certain level. If you want to go for the gold, you want to connect to the dreams and desires that are rooted in love, that come from your heart.

Dreams from the Influence of Others Versus Dreams from Your Heart

As you begin the self-inquiry into what you want, I invite you to be very intentional in connecting with your genuine wants instead of what your mind may be replaying of others' opinions and wants for you. Trying to live someone else's dream for you is like being under the influence of drugs or caffeine: sooner or later, the effects will wear off and you will wake up. The question is would you still want the same career and life when you "wake up"?

My encouragement for you is to cultivate a connection to the dreams that are truly yours. I was speaking to a woman in her late forties who had a very successful career in technology. However, she had always been an artist as well, and a very talented one. Even though she had never made a penny with her art up to that point, although she easily could have, she devoted years of her life to mastering the craft, and she lit up every time we talked about it. No matter what would happen at her place of employment or with her family, doing art was her heartfelt, authentic desire that gave her strength to work through many life challenges.

I invite you to begin connecting to desires like that. Once you do, you will become unstoppable because you become powered from a very different source; you become powered by the authentic desire that comes directly from your heart.

It may not be easy to distill our authentic desires from the ones we have picked up from the others. Here is one version of an exercise that I often do with my clients.

First, I ask them to pick something that they think they want, and then I ask them to answer the following questions:

- Describe what it is that you want to have/be/do/ experience?
- Why do you want it? What do you hope it will bring you? What else? What else?
- When you imagine yourself having/being/doing what you want, how does it feel in your body? Do you feel expansive or constricted? Warm, cold? Are you aware of any emotions?
- What is the quality of the experience that you want?
- Who are you trying to please if you achieve your goal? Or impress?
- How committed are you to this goal/want/desire?
- Do you have any judgments of this desire/want?

My wish for you is to slow down to connect to the deeper want, the one that is yours and is not a "hallucination" from the influence of the family, the culture, the bodily desires, or the mood. Once the connection to your genuine desire/dream is made, you will be surprised at how fast your life begins to move and you will create at levels that you didn't think were possible!

Remove Self-Imposed Caps on Dreams

As you begin to connect to the dreams that are authentically yours, most of you will hit another challenge of realizing that you may have forgotten how to dream without limits. Hence comes the next tool – removing any caps or limitations that you may have placed on your capacity to dream and claim what you want.

Dreaming, wanting, and asking for what you want is a very natural process. If you don't believe me, just observe a child under the age of six. Most kids connect to what they want very easily, and they are not afraid to ask for it. They are also dreaming big and are not worried about their dreams "being realistic" or "making any sense." A kid can share that she wants to be an astronaut and a writer or a ballerina and a business owner all in one breath. Everything is possible, and no limits are created. Can you imagine a child saying to another child, "I want to pick a job based on my skills that pays the bills so that I can be responsible"? A child feels very hurt when an adult denies her wants. I am not a child psychologist; however, for the purposes of coaching clients to connect and to embody their big dreams, I found it very useful to first reconnect to their capacity to dream and to retrain themselves to ask for what they want.

In my experience, most clients who come in saying that they want more clarity have a deeper sense of what they really want to do; however, they are blocking themselves from hearing themselves, scaring themselves too early. However, the authentic dreams do not shut up and they do not go away. Trust me on this one. So, my invitation is to begin to listen. I often encourage clients to begin gently by giving themselves permission to dream "crazy dreams" and allow all kinds of ideas to come forward without any commitment to any action. I even have some clients write their own permission slip to explore and dream and get messy.

I remember hearing a story about Steve Jobs and how he was recruiting for the team that eventually created the first iPhone. He was looking for individuals who were willing and excited about spending each day getting messy, trying new things, and failing most of the time, knowing they would create something great.

Most of the clients share how as they were growing up, they were trained to think that dreams had to be sensible and that the clients were supposed to look good and polished at least most of the time on the way to their goals. However, in my experience, the biggest successes, the role models who disrupt and transform the world of business, arts, and technology, the ones who succeed not only in the office but also in their personal life, are the ones who are not afraid to dream big; the ones who connect to what they really want (not what their parents or friends want for them), and then take risks, get messy, fail, adjust, and then rise and create a professional expression that nobody could have imagined before.

The problem is that it is tempting to look at these individuals and think that when they took the first step, they knew they were going to wear a designer suit and speak on big stages in seven years. However, they didn't. They had an inkling, a dream, and a commitment. They had a willingness to lean it.

I remember speaking to a woman from upstate New York who was close friends with Jimmy Fallon since she and Jimmy were in their early twenties. Back then, Jimmy had a vision of being on *Saturday Night Live*, but his reality at the time was doing stand-up routines at a local bar with barely anybody there. The woman and her family would go and support him. So many years later, she would see him on *Saturday Night Live* and, then, *The Tonight Show* and reflect on his success and how he had started powered by only a dream and simply kept showing up.

Everyone starts small. Even those who seem to hit the jackpot early go through the process of facing their fears and insecurities and being willing to show up without any guarantees of success. However, the key with dreaming big is to not limit yourself with what you see around you. In other words, if I want to be an inspirational public speaker, but the current reality is that I choke every time I share any personal stories at the local Toastmasters club (which is where I started years ago), then I can keep showing up and growing while allowing myself to dream and see myself teaching and inspiring the audiences from the big stage. That big dream is there for a reason. It is the North Star. Most people lose track of their North Star. My intention for this chapter is to support you in connecting to yours.

Reclaim Your Right to Dream Big

I often take clients through an exercise of reflecting on their relationship to dreaming. I ask them questions such as:

- How often to you give yourself permission to dream or really want something?
- How often do you ask for something that you want?

- How willing are you to receive?
- What are your fears or hesitations around dreaming?
- How do you stop yourself from dreaming?
- How often do you remind yourself to be realistic before you had a chance to connect to something that you want?

It is common for tears to show up as clients recall painful incidences from their past when they got really disappointed by not achieving their dream and, because of that, stopped themselves from ever wanting something so deeply again.

It makes complete sense to numb the pain. In the short term, that may work fine. However, the long-term price tag is very high. It is like having a drink to relax. As a short-term solution for some people, it may be effective; however, if taken to an extreme and used as a daily practice, one can numb himself to the point of not being able to connect to any of his authentic wants.

When I was learning various therapy techniques during my studies for my master's in spiritual psychology, I observed over and over again that when a client numbs her negative feelings and emotions, she also numbs her positive feelings and emotions. The same goes for dreaming. If a client start numbing his daily wants, it becomes difficult to connect to his bigger dreams on demand. He becomes more and more reliant on what the culture or family tells him he wants.

My invitation for you here is to begin to connect to the authentic wanting and to begin to uncap any limits and untangle any negative associations you may have placed on wanting something with your whole heart.

The next tool that I want to introduce is beginning to identify your own unique blend of fears that have been putting a cap on your authentic desires and wants and to begin dissolving them or, at least, working more intentionally with them.

Fight Fears around Dreaming Big

These are some of the most common fears that my clients share when we go deeper into this subject:

- I am afraid of getting disappointed and not being able to handle the pain.
- I am afraid of being rejected.
- I am afraid of losing face.
- I am afraid of being seen as a failure.
- I am afraid that wanting is not spiritual.
- I am afraid that wanting is selfish.
- I am afraid that if I allow myself to want that I will never have enough.
- I am afraid that if I allow myself to want I will need to change and leave the life that is familiar to me behind.
- I am afraid that if I allow myself to want and to go for what I want I would be selfish and ungrateful to my parents, who sacrificed so much for me.
- I am afraid to offend or upset others by going for what I want.

- I am afraid of not being good enough to go for what I want.
- I am afraid that I cannot make enough money doing what I love.

The list keeps going. What is your flavor of the fear bundle?

Here is the next question – how is listening to these fears serving you? How is it working out for you? What is the price tag that you are paying?

Fears activate the part of our brain called amygdala, which is the most primitive part of a human brain. It is the part that triggers fight/flight/freeze response and has no access to the logical or the creative type of thought. None! So this part is not equipped to think or process information. This is why if you allow fears to activate that part of your brain, it becomes very challenging to rationally talk your way out of something, because the part of the brain that is activated is *not* the thinking part.

Mel Robbins has shared a lot on this subject in her talks about the five-second rule. If you are not familiar, I recommend her talks, including her TED talk. But the premise is that when we are in fear, the prefrontal part of our brain, which is the thinking part, is not activated. In order to activate it, she suggests counting backward – 5, 4, 3, 2, 1 – and then leap into action. If you are curious, give it a try.

I found that moving your body can also work to disrupt the fear. Or another technique that can be supportive is Tapping or EFT (Emotional Freedom Technique). There are many coaches who work with it as the primary focus, if you want to look it up. I love its simplicity and the diversity of application.

I will share many more tools on working with the fears and the limiting beliefs in Chapters 8 and 9 when I share stories and examples on how to align mind and emotions and working with resistance. To give you a preview, there is a lot of power in training yourself to prevent that part of the brain from being activated; it is very much trainable. This process begins with awareness of the most repetitive thoughts that occupy your mind. These thoughts are usually not very creative. So for now, I invite you to begin to notice and journal the most common fears that you identify with. Then, once you get to the chapters on resistance and aligning emotions and mind, you can go deeper into dissolving the fears.

Chapter Highlights

- It is imperative and very useful to train yourself to distinguish between the wants and desires that come from the influence of others and the ones that are authentically yours.
- Connecting to the dreams that are rooted in love and that are authentically yours super charges you for success.
- Most clients that I see put limits and caps on what they allow themselves to want and to ask for. In some ways, they reject their dreams before anybody else has a chance to. And then they claim that they don't have clarity on what to do next, but the truth is that many of them are afraid to claim what they truly want and need support in this area.

- I invite you to become aware of your unique fear bundle as it relates to dreaming and going for what you want. Begin to notice how these fears impact your daily choices and decision-making.

Suggested Next Steps and Exercises

- Begin to train yourself to develop awareness of when your want is authentically yours versus when it is more of a flavor of the hour/day/month that is coming from an outside influence and will naturally dissolve.
- Go through the questions around putting limits on wanting. What are your limits? Do you allow yourself to dream?
- You can choose to run an experiment for a week or a month of daily asking for something that you want. Make it fun! And journal about how you felt before, during, and after.
- Go through the list of common fears and reflect on the ones that you are aware of. Which fears are the most prevalent for you? Write them down, so that you can recognize them when they come in. You will have a chance to work more with dissolving fears later in the book.

* * *

Congratulations on making it through this chapter. I realize connecting to fears and reflecting on your previous disappointments and limitations may not be comfortable and, honestly, often is quite painful. Many of the clients in my groups have a lot of fears and anxieties come up at this stage that we address together. If that is the case for you, you may want to take a break from reading and watch a complimentary video master class on *How to Handle Fear Effectively*. You can watch the class at any time as you are working through the book, when you want additional support.

You can download it here: clearwaycoach.com/free

* * *

Now that you have poked around enough and hopefully untangled some tight knots around wanting, desires, and limitations, in the next chapter you will have an opportunity to slow down and have lots of fun with creating a vision that is a Sacred YES for you.

Chapter 5:

Enlist a Vision That Is a Sacred YES!

"Nothing is impossible, the word itself
says 'I'm possible'!"
— **Audrey Hepburn**

"The future belongs to those who believe in
the beauty of their dreams."
— **Eleanor Roosevelt**

"At the center of your being you have the answer.
You know who you are and you know what you want."
— **Lao Tzu**

Choose the Direction

There is a famous quote that "a journey of a thousand miles begins with the single step." I love it. It is very romantic. However, it is important that we choose the direction first, because there is also another saying – no matter how high we climb, it is all for nothing if the ladder is being placed next to the wrong wall.

In my experience, there is a lot of value in attuning early on and choosing the direction to begin taking steps that reflect a Sacred YES for you. I define a Sacred YES as when you know with the core of your being that this decision is a yes. It could feel exciting, or terrifying or anything else in between, but there is a certain type of inner resonance, a gut feeling, and a knowing that is bigger than logic.

I am not being romantic here. I am being very practical. The more you can train the skill of attuning to what is a Sacred YES to you, the yes that is beyond the pros/cons list, the easier and more smoothly you will proceed forward in all areas of your life, especially professionally.

So how do you do it? How do you train yourself to connect to your Sacred YES vision?

In order to do that, I will take you through several exercises/ stepping-stones that I often take clients through. Each one is meant to contribute and elevate you higher and higher, so that you can see where you are going, metaphorically speaking.

Collect Clues and Ideas

The first exercise that I like to offer to my clients is to share about two or three people whom they are inspired by. Clients talk about big stars, leaders, colleagues, friends, and parents. And then I invite them to dive deeper into what exactly inspires them about these people. Is it what they do? Is it how they show up? What qualities are extra juicy and inspiring?

I remember when I first did this exercise many years ago, I came up with three people: Robert Holden, Marianne Williamson, and Louise Hay. All three are authors, speakers, and teachers (Louise Hay has passed away since then, but she started a revolution in the self-development field, including publishing several books and eventually starting a publishing house and she didn't begin until after she turned sixty.). What moved me about my role models were the depth of their work and impact, their heart-centeredness, their willingness to serve, their courage and vulnerability, their way of connecting in such an authentic way, and how much they cared about their readers and students. I also was inspired by their qualities of character, courage, vulnerability, openness and devotion to being a student, devotion to spiritual practices, willingness to keep showing up to teach, their caring, and their loving hearts. I also really admired how productive they were while also focusing on enjoying a rich personal life with their families, friends, and loved ones; their focus on joy; their appreciation of life; and their connection to others. I am feeling inspired even right now as I am recalling and capturing these qualities.

Once the clients complete their lists of what inspires them about their role models, we begin to analyze their findings in the context of choosing a professional path. It does not always translate one to one. For example, I have many clients who mention Oprah as their inspiration, but here is the key:

everyone talks about what they find most inspiring in different ways. I had one client talk about Oprah's courage to keep going until she changed the system and broke so many invisible glass ceilings. I had another client talk about Oprah's productivity and creativity, how she continues coming up with various ways to serve and to have greater and greater impact. I had yet another client talk about Oprah's resiliency, her dedication and devotion to what she believed in, her strong voice. Each client was moved by the different things, so the key is to go a few layers deep.

For me, in the earlier example, I became more clear on how much I wanted to serve others in a way that was empowering, inspiring, and liberating to those I worked with. I also very practically became more aware of what I deep down already knew about how much I wanted to serve by writing and publishing a book that was deeply meaningful to me and how much I loved coaching and teaching. There is a lot of wisdom in this one exercise, and if you give yourself time to go deeper here without any expectations, full of innocent curiosity, there are a lot of gems of clarity that could be found in plain sight.

Sometimes when clients are having a hard time connecting to their inspirational figures, I invite them to research and bring some pictures of the people who inspire them, their quotes or stories about them so that the client can begin to connect to what touches them more deeply. It is so much fun, and the clients always leave elevated and inspired.

You May Be Further Along Than You Realize

The first part of the exercise helps clients to get clearer about some of their experiences, inner and outer, that they may want to cultivate in their lives. Then the next step of the exercise is to focus on the qualities of character that the inspirational figure has and begin to cultivate these qualities in themselves.

Let me give you an example. I remember one client talking about Oprah's leadership, vision, and drive. I asked her if she had ever demonstrated these qualities in any area of her life in her thirty-two years. She said, "Well, yes, of course." And she shared a situation, but then she quickly added, "But I am not really a leader." I invited her to slow down and share more. (Coaches love to invite clients to slow down!) She shared more specifics, finally acknowledging that she obviously demonstrated these qualities, hence they were already active in her. She recognized that what she really wanted was a greater mastery and demonstration of her leadership and courage. We then looked at her leadership and courage as a spectrum from 0 to 100 (the scale can be anything). And she identified that she was at about 20 and she thought she needed to be at 80 to start and grow her business. We then discussed how she could connect with her existing leadership quality and the quality of courage and expand them both. That was a powerful exercise for her, and she dove into action that week with lots of enthusiasm. In many ways, her focusing on growing her leadership was an essential step moving her toward her Sacred YES vision.

The key takeaway here is that it is a lot easier and fun to grow something that you know you already have versus focusing on acquiring a brand-new quality. In my experience, this change in context is often incredibly powerful in facilitating growth, motivation, and commitment.

Connect with the Deeper Goal Underneath the Goal

Once we identify the areas and qualities that are most inspiring to a client, we often go back to the heartfelt desires that the client has connected with in the earlier exercises, this time mostly focusing on the quality of experience that he really wants. For example, one of my clients, George, is a powerful coach who is growing his practice. When he first came to me, he wanted to work on increasing his client base and his revenue, which were clear and useful goals. However, when we dove a bit deeper to what the quality of the experience that he really wanted was, he recognized that he wanted to connect to others, heart to heart, and have a big and positive impact on everyone he gets to work with. Once he connected to his deeper goals, his eyes lit up. He stood up taller and the ideas that started pouring out of him were incredibly expansive and inspiring.

Clients come in with all kinds of dreams. I encourage them to identify the dream that is underneath the dream, the goal under the goal, not the surface goal, but the one that is half-hidden and driving the whole show. Once they identify and connect to that goal/dream, the clients become unstoppable.

Remember that desires and dreams that come from "under the influence" of the culture or the people in your life dissolve like smoke and cannot sustain you or anyone else under pressure; however, once you connect to the dreams that are rooted in your heart, your authentic desires, you can always come back to them to refuel. You get access to an unlimited supply of inspiration, energy, and perseverance. So, if you are still not sure what your deeper intention is, you may want to reflect on the following questions and search for qualities of experience or qualities of character. Some questions to reflect on include:

- What is it that I really, really, really want?
- Why do I want it?
- What do I hope to experience if I have it?
- What else? What else? What else?

Usually at this point a client will have many more ideas that are exciting and at least some tingling desires for which direction they want to pursue. I usually don't encourage anyone to lock themselves into any direction. It is great when a client shares that they are now clear and they want X. However, most clients will typically be excited by several possibilities at this stage, the level of enthusiasm is much higher than before, and the possible directions are fewer and more defined.

Try on Dream Jobs and Visions for "Size"

The next tool that I often use at this stage is inviting a client to create a vision or several potential visions of what her entire life would look like if she were to lean in and be successful in each one of the chosen directions. Most of clients forget that their work life has to fit into their personal life. In my experience, it doesn't matter how successful a client becomes, if she is not happy with the other parts of her life, she will get antsy for a change.

There are many ways to connect to the bigger vision, depending on the amount of time and energy that a person wants to spend and how they like to think/reflect. With some clients, I lead them through a process of creating a mind map of different areas of her life and what her life would look like if she were to choose a particular direction.

With other clients who are more kinesthetic, I take them through a process of embodying their potential career and taking them forward into several years from now and inviting them to connect to their Future Self and share what they are noticing, what does their life look like, how does it feel. It is incredible to watch what comes up.

Yet with other clients, who like crafts, I invite them to collect pictures, quotes, and affirmations and create vision boards of what they want to experience.

Yet for others, we do something similar by creating an ideal scene or ideal vision but with descriptions only. The possibilities are endless here. The key intention for all the exercises is to facilitate a connection to the possible future and basically "try it on for size." In my experience, our bodies cannot lie, so we know instantly if something is "off." And it is great when we get that feedback. So we can course correct right away.

Get to Know Your Future Self

The clients, at this point, are usually much clearer about the direction or at least about what they want to experience, so the next exercise that I take them through is getting to know the person that they will need to become to live their future vision of success. What is she like? How does she spend her days? How does she take care of herself? What are her priorities? What does she say "yes" to? What does she say "no" to? Who does she spend time with?

This is a very eye-opening exercise for most of the clients that I have worked with, as they begin to notice in what ways they are already a match to this person of future success and where they have opportunities for growth. Naturally, the client begins to self-identify opportunities in his current life where he can step more fully and be the person of the future success.

One short exercise that I often do is identifying what the client wants to say yes and no to in her life now from the perspective of her Future Self. It leads to effortless clarity in ways that most clients do not expect and many begin to use "what would my Future Self do in this situation?" as a reference point for making decisions. This becomes incredibly effective for connecting to the state of inner clarity that we talked about in Chapter 3.

Another great question that I often offer to my clients to reflect on is "What can I do today to more fully embody my Future Self?".

Each time you ask this question it will generate many ideas for possible action steps, and it is so much fun to take them.

The Art of Choosing Next Steps

Once a client becomes more comfortable connecting and working with her Future Self, another popular exercise that I offer is to begin inviting the Future Self to pick the next steps. Let me share the story of one of my clients, Mary. Mary was going to an interview, and she knew the HR person and her prospective boss preferred that she worked fifty hours a week. Her Future Self was very clear that she wanted to work no more than thirty-five hours a week. When Mary was getting ready for the interview, she became overwhelmed and felt confused and lost in fear of speaking up, fear of being rejected, and fear of losing an opportunity that she really wanted. Thankfully, we connected for a coaching call the day before the interview, and I invited Mary to revisit her Future Self who was working thirty-five hours a week and ask her what she would recommend to do in this situation. Mary let her Future Self come forward and then listened in silence. Within a minute, she was sharing alternative options for how she could negotiate with her prospective boss regarding working fewer hours. She also noticed that she felt less attached and more open to looking for a completely different job, if needed. She then had an idea to offer a plan to her prospective boss for how she could begin working fifty hours a week but with half of those hours being remote and to later slowly step down to thirty-five hours a week over six months to a year. Mary's eyes were sparkling, and the possibilities seemed to be endless after our discussion.

I have never seen a client who is truly connected to her Future Self become lost or confused. There seems to always be an answer, and it is often surprising!

Albert Einstein said, "We can't solve problems by using the same kind of thinking we used when we created them."

The reason this exercise is so effective is that you connect to the thinking pattern that is different from the one that created the state of confusion. You allow the new, higher level of thinking come up with the solution.

I invite you to play with connecting and getting to know your Future Self and with trying on various visions for size. It is such a fun and effective way to get clear answers and move into action!

Chapter Highlights

- Reflecting on who inspires you and why holds many clues for what you may want to experience in your career and personal life.
- You already possess the qualities that you are inspired by in others, so you can begin to nurture these qualities as a first step in moving forward toward living your Sacred YES vision.
- Connecting to your deeper goal behind the goal is imperative for not only choosing a direction for your career that is authentic but also for refueling you as you move forward and hit the inevitable resistance (more on dissolving resistance in later chapters).

- As the vision becomes clearer, it is very helpful to ask, "What kind of person do I need to become to live this vision?"
- Let the Future Self, the wiser version of you, who is already clear on your career and success, guide your next steps.

Suggested Next Steps and Exercises

- Pick two to three people who inspire you and list what moves you and why.
- Ask yourself how you have demonstrated the qualities that you admire in others.
- If nurturing some of the previously mentioned qualities is key to your success, ask yourself, "How can I further grow and develop this quality that I already have and lean into action?"
- Reconnect to your deeper intention underneath your goals. Allow the deeper intentions to continue to guide you in choosing your direction. Answer the questions about what is it that you really, really want? What is the quality of the experience that you want? What does it feel to experience this level of wanting? How does it feel in your body? What thoughts are present? Any emotions? Physical sensations? Write these qualities/intentions on sticky notes or any other ways and remind yourself often. Give your intentions your attention.

- Journal about what kind of a person you would need to become to be the person living your vision of success. What can you do to move in that direction today?
- Create a vision for how your ideal work fits into the life that you want to live and visit it often. I like to hang my vision pictures on the fridge. It is very uplifting to see, and I effortlessly connect with my vision daily every time I open the fridge.
- During your mindfulness practice from Chapter 3, set the intention to connect to the Future Self of success and ask her/him for guidance regarding the next steps and then listen and journal the answers that you get. If you do this daily, you will soon notice some themes and once you do, you can choose to test out some of these action steps.

* * *

This was a very full chapter with many exercises and a lot to take in. I spend a fair amount of time with clients going through these stages, and I acknowledge you for your openness to receive these tools in a condensed and very concentrated version in the book. I invite you to take some time to digest.

Once you are ready, in the next chapter, you will discover your own unique formula for success that will support you with taking action the most effectively.

Chapter 6:

Access Your Personal Success Formula

"Vision is not enough; it must be combined with
venture. It is not enough to stare up the steps;
we must step up the stairs."
— VACLAV HAVEL

Move Forward to Stay Clear

Most clients who come in thinking that they need to get
clearer on their vision often discover that what they essentially
crave for is to take action but feel stuck.

In this chapter, I will be sharing tools for how to move into action by first discovering your own unique recipe for success. I call it your "personal success formula".

No two individuals are exactly alike; however, when it comes down to searching or giving advice for how to be successful, most approaches seem to favor one path that is somehow magically supposed to fit everyone. Well, in my experience, most of my clients are too dynamic for one path, regardless of how brilliant this path may be. So instead of copying someone else's formula, I take the clients on a journey of discovering their own unique success path.

The good news is you already have a recipe for success that you have tested and experimented with, so all you need to do is to bring it out and make it more accessible and usable for the purposes of choosing what to do and proceeding with the next action steps.

This chapter is also the first of several chapters that I have included in the book to support you with creating a unique and practical framework to become a lot more aware of how you personally make decisions and commitments and how you achieve success. I invite you to slow down and to really take in each concept in one at a time and to experiment with the exercise suggestions as you discover and fine-tune your personal success formula.

You will begin by learning the basics of the action loops and how they work. You will then go deeper into discerning between practices for short-term success and long-term success. Then you will explore how you make decisions and commitments, which will support you with getting to know what moves you to action. All of these elements will help you become even more aware of your success formula, which you will outline by the end of the chapter. As a bonus, I will also introduce a tool for managing your time and projects that may be surprising and is very effective with most clients I have worked with.

Adjust the Action Loop for Maximum Success

The first concept that I want to introduce is an overview of an action/feedback loop. Some of you may be familiar with it and some of you are probably not. Most of clients that I have worked with shared a linear way of looking at action/feedback loops:

I get clear on my vision > I take action > If I like the feedback that I receive after taking the action step – great, I keep going! If I don't like the feedback from the action step, then I decide that I had made a mistake when I was getting clear, so I need to go back to square one and reevaluate my initial vision.

In other words, if the action doesn't work out, I take that as a feedback to stop moving and a sign that I need to reexamine the direction of the original vision.

There is nothing wrong here; however, it may not be the most effective way to work with the action/feedback loop. The problem here is that this type of thinking assumes that if an action does not produce the result that I was expecting, then the entire vision must have been a mistake and I should stop. I hear so many stories of people who stop so early on their paths that they never lift their dream off the ground.

As an alternative, let me share the action/feedback loop that I found to work a lot more effectively:

I get clear on my vision > I take an action step > I get feedback based on the action that I took > I reflect/analyze and incorporate feedback and adjust the type of action as needed > I take more action >>>> I keep moving toward my vision.

Notice that in this scenario I am actively using feedback that I am receiving to keep refining the action plan and moving forward, when in the first scenario the feedback was misused to create a roadblock to doubt the entire vision and to stop taking action.

Let me give you an example of how this may look by analyzing a situation where one of the most common fears shows up: the fear of rejection.

Let's say I want to get a speaking gig at a national career conference. I create my speaker's bio, outline the talk, and pitch it to the organizer. I am all excited and make a request to speak, and I get a "no." In the first action/feedback loop scenario, I most likely will take the "no" and tell myself that it was a mistake to even apply, that I cannot trust my inspiration and desire to be a speaker, and that the desire is probably all wrong. The best case is that I may try out for a smaller gig elsewhere. In this scenario, what I see frequently is that this person may stop completely and stick to speaking at her local Toastmasters group and free community events. And there is nothing wrong here – in many ways, this used to be me a number of years ago – and yet there is so much more available here.

Let's take the same situation and take it through the second loop of action/feedback. Same guidance and inspiration: I apply to speak and get a "no." This time I receive it as a feedback on my action of pitching and not on my initial guidance and inspiration to be a speaker.

In this situation, I reflect and get curious. What may be another way to either make my service more relatable to this organizer or maybe find another venue that is more appropriate? That is, I analyze feedback constructively so it generates more action ideas and keeps the momentum going. Let's say as I am analyzing this feedback, I am noticing that I still feel inspired to speak at this career conference or at a similar event, so I lean into reaching out and hiring a coach who helps speakers grow their business and learn the proper marketing tools. Or I may get an inspiration to reconnect with the organizer and ask if she would be willing to spend fifteen minutes on the phone to share what she is looking for if I choose to reapply for next year. Or I may get inspired to go through my network and see if there is anyone else that I know who is speaking and see if I can take them out for lunch and ask for advice. Notice, I am still connected to my vision in the second scenario, and I stay in action when in the first scenario I stopped.

It is very exciting to see once a client has her "aha!" moment and sees the power in working with the action loop. I invite you to give it a try and choose for yourself.

Power Up Your Success Formula

The next reminder that I like to give to my clients as they begin to work with their success formula is to be very intentional about incorporating "good feeling states" such as joy, love, peace – whatever the most juicy and inspiring qualities are – into their success formula. This is imperative for multiple reasons. It is obviously a lot more fun to take action when the journey is enjoyable. However, there is a lot more practical reasoning behind here that I want to share. As I have mentioned in earlier chapters, fear can be a powerful motivator. However, fear can only take you so far. I have seen clients achieve a fair amount of success being motivated by fear; however, unless they switch their source of "power" to joy, love, meaning or similar they will eventually burn out. That is why we hear so many stories of people in all kinds of fields, from business to entertainment, who achieve an incredible level of success and then can't seem to enjoy it and often act out to sabotage it. Fear works, but it is a very expensive coach and everyone who uses and relies on it will inevitably have to pay a price.

Love (i.e. connecting to something that you enjoy that feels bigger that you), on the other hand, pays you dividends, so when you use love as the motivator you can keep going and feeling refueled by the action itself. This is why early in the process I spend a fair amount of time with my clients supporting them in connecting to their deeper dreams that are coming from their hearts, instead of fears. You are here for the long haul, and love is such a fun and generous companion. I invite you to jump on board!

The Art of Making and Keeping Commitments

Making commitments and following through is a very hot topic and there is a lot of advice out there on the best way to do so. In my experience of working with all kinds of clients, I have yet to see two people who have the same process of making decisions. So my invitation for all of my clients is to take time to get to know how they make decisions and what is their relationship with commitment, as I know it will ultimately serve them for the rest of their lives.

With that intention in mind I take the clients through several exercises. One includes identifying and sharing several stories when the client made decisions and clear choices, including making commitments that worked out very well. We then analyze the contributing factors. Was it a commitment to someone else? What motivated the client to make the commitment and what motivated the client to keep her word? How did the client show up and support herself to keep the agreement? Was it challenging to keep or was it easy? What got in the way and how did she respond?

Here is what came up for me when I recently revisited this exercise. When I give my word several things happen. In most instances, I keep my word, however in a few rare instances I don't. What I realized is that I usually know deep in my gut (remember inner coach/intuition) as I am giving my word, if I am going to keep it. In a rare instance that I feel "off" when I make a commitment, I notice that I feel a disturbance in my gut. If I still proceed with saying "yes", then I usually notice that I either find myself breaking the agreement, renegotiating it later, or admitting that I didn't really want to make it and default on it. So the learning here for me is to pay attention to how I feel when I first make the commitment. If I take it a step further, I can ask, "Why do I choose to make the commitments that feels off?" For me, a frequent answer used to be people pleasing so that I felt loved and accepted more and so that I could avoid feeling bad when disappointing others by saying "no". Notice as I dig deeper, I can do more healing work around the underlying desire to feel more lovable and the fear of disappointing others to shift those patterns. As I do, I will find that it becomes significantly easier to make *only* the agreements that I know in my core I will keep.

There can be multiple reasons for someone to make commitments that don't feel good. One other example that was very present for me a few years ago was to prove to myself that I am enough and can handle it all. I will go deeper into this and similar toxic misunderstandings later in the book. I don't want to jump too far ahead, but if you find that you have a lot of question marks come up for you during this process, you may want to pause and browse through Chapter 9, where I share tools on aligning the mind and emotions, and come back to this chapter once you have worked through some of that material.

When I identify how I feel when I make commitments that I won't keep, I am noticing a physical sensation of something being off. I have awareness that I have some insecurities that I am trying to cover up by making a commitment that doesn't feel 100 percent right. Notice I am not judging anything, I am observing as neutrally as I can.

On the other hand, when I make a commitment that feels great, I notice that I keep it and that it is very easy to keep, there is no drama, and I seem to be very clear on my priorities.

So for me, in order to ensure that I kept my commitments, I focused on coaching myself through the insecurities that used to lead to making agreements that I did not genuinely want to make, stopping myself, and/or backing out of agreements that I didn't feel good about, even if that meant temporarily upsetting other people. Notice, it was not a magical pill; however, it proved to be a very effective path given my previous patterns.

Some clients listen to the stories that I share and tell me that they have the best of intentions when they make their commitments to keep them, but then something better comes along and they can't seem to choose. Or they have emergencies come up, and they can't keep their original commitment or they lose interest. Some reason to break the commitment comes up.

In these situations, I invite the client to slow down and replay an instance when they made a commitment that did not work out and what happened as they made it. A fun way to do this is to imagine that moment being replayed on a giant movie screen in front of you in very slow motion.

What usually happens is that the client begins to share how they felt excitement when they got a clear "yes"; they were motivated for the first few days or weeks, but then the resistance kicked in and their commitment wavered. In this situation, we would work on the tools for dealing with the resistance. I cover tool for working with resistance in Chapter 8, "Wire Resistance to Work for You."

In a similar situation, the client shares that she seems to lose enthusiasm and can't keep her commitments. In this case, we look at what fueled the commitment to begin with. Let me give you an example. A coach in her early forties wanted to grow her new coaching practice. However, she seemed to lose her interest and felt very guilty about breaking her weekly commitments to herself regarding connecting with the prospective clients. We slowed down and went back to the foundations and reconnected with her deeper intention. She went deeper than ever before, as she now had a lot more awareness from coaching, and she saw that her deeper intention was to create a stream of income that would give her freedom to travel and to write. What she really wanted was to travel and write and have a living that would allow her to do that. No wonder her commitment to coaching wasn't strong. It came from her idea of a limitation, as she originally couldn't imagine what else she could be doing using her skills to give her that freedom in life. What was interesting is that once she saw the deeper intention, she made a commitment to the vision of creating a life where she could travel and write. She let go of it needing it to be about coaching or anything else. Ironically, later she found herself getting excited about coaching again and began leading virtual groups and retreats, all while writing and traveling.

When I work with clients on making decisions, I invite them to "embody" their prospective decisions and commitments before they say "yes" or "no." Embodying in this context means to notice any feelings in the body. Our bodies cannot lie, the best they can do is numb. So, as you are making a commitment and saying "yes", you will feel something. It may be very subtle but you will feel it. Train yourself to notice. Does it feel expansive and warm, or does it feel like a drop or punch in the gut and constrictive? Notice your version of a clear "yes" and a clear "no." I promise everyone has it. The clients who train themselves to only make commitments that feel expansive notice that it becomes much easier to keep their commitments, even when the resistance and roadblocks show up. This level of attunement and integrity with your word before you ever give your word takes time to cultivate and I promise you, it will serve you for the rest of your life.

I haven't talked too much about exploring what commitments mean to you. It could be a very eye-opening exercise, so if you notice yourself resisting making any kind of commitments or if you always find yourself breaking commitments or feel frozen by the fear of making a wrong choice, I invite you to journal your observations and use the additional tools in Chapters 8 and 9 on resistance and aligning your mind and emotions to work through them.

Stay Inspired for Action

Now that we have talked about making decisions and commitments, the next part of the puzzle is to identify what inspires you to action. I love to be inspired and motivated by someone else! However, if you want to move forward in a consistent matter, you cannot depend on a flimsy unpredictable waves of moods and inspirations that life may offer you. So the next set of exercises that I often offer to my clients is to slow down to evaluate what truly moves them to action, which is different from what makes them feel comfortable (and potentially sit on the couch).

There are many ways to do this and we often begin with a conversation about the last time the client took action on a big project to discuss what moved him or her to action. Same as with the goal setting, sometimes the motivator is a fear of a negative consequence and sometimes it is a calling that is powered by love, such as a desire to support a friend. The first step is to identify what typically inspires you to move to action and write it down.

I will give you an example, I have a client who is motivated by serving, connecting and also by having deadlines. So for her, she had a really hard time motivating herself until she finally committed and started working with several clients. She became so moved by her clients that, even though her calendar got fuller and fuller, she kept sharing how much more energy and motivation for creative action she had experienced.

I have another client who was originally motivated by fear of losing her husband if she didn't change. It was a fear-based motivation, but it worked well for her to at least to help get her through the door of my office. Once we began working together, she used that original motivation to get her started, and then she dug more to connect to the underlying yearning to experience deeper intimacy with her husband and with herself and also to empower others. The revised motivation kept her powered up even more effortlessly.

The key is to find out what motivates you and to use it intentionally.

Discover Your Personal Success Formula

Once you have identified what motivates you to action, you are ready for the next step. I love doing this exercise with clients as it creates so many exciting possibilities and greatly accelerates their progress.

I begin by letting a client recall a story of success from her life. It could be a professional success or a personal success. Sometimes we look at a couple or more stories of success. And once the client shares the success story in sufficient detail, I invite her to identify the key attributes around this experience. They may or may not be related.

Let me give you an example. Let's say a client had been successful in landing a great job out of college with over $100,000 salary. We slow down and look at how she showed up in her success.

She identifies that she was having fun, she was unattached to the outcome, she was present, she was curious, she did the homework to prepare and get to know more about the company, she listened to her gut, she drank water and took her vitamins and had a good night sleep before the interview; she also had a great conversation with her friend the morning before the interview that was uplifting. Notice that we are listing all kinds of attributes. Once we do, we can look at another success story that this client had and evaluate if any of the attributes overlapped. They often do. The attributes that overlap are some of the core components of the client's success recipe, and the more the client is aware of them, the more she can intentionally re-create the recipe and apply it to accelerate her progress. And it is so much fun to do. It becomes a very exciting game!

Keys for Effective Time and Project Management

I have covered a lot in this chapter already, but I promised you a bonus, so here it is! At this stage, clients often become focused on how to organize their calendar and their projects to support themselves with their goals. And the intention is a genuine desire to be more effective; however, let me share a secret. The most successful clients that I have worked with do not focus on organizing their time or a to-do list to maximize productivity. They focus on how to organize themselves for maximum results. It is a very different focus.

Let me explain what I mean. I had a client who is a business owner, and he was testing out different ways to schedule his work time on his calendar. He tried to-do lists that were very long and aggressive and tested out blocking work hours on his calendar, but he still would come up short at the end of the week in reaching his goals. Then one week, he shifted away from the essential question, "How do I need to organize my calendar" to another essential question: "How do I need to organize myself to reach my goals?" And everything changed. He simplified his goals from a long list of over a dozen for a week, to having a goal of hitting three key benchmarks daily. He also worked deeply with connecting and using what motivated him to pick his activities for the workday, instead of focusing on "logging in time." His business took off shortly after this change.

You are going deeper and deeper into the journey toward taking action from a place of a Sacred YES, and I acknowledge you for being willing to keep going. I often tell my clients that this journey is not for a faint of heart and requires a lot of courage.

Chapter Highlights

- Choosing how you interpret and work with the feedback via the action loop can either stop you early in the process or can support you in moving toward your goals more smoothly. The clients who have been the most successful have been using this version of the action loop: *I get clear on my vision > I take an action step > I get feedback based on the action that I took > I reflect/analyze and incorporate feedback and adjust the type of action as needed > I take more action >>>> I keep moving toward my vision.*

- "Power up" your success formula by being intentional with cultivating "good feeling states" as a part of the long-term success strategy.

- As you get more familiar with how you make decisions and commitments by listening to the inner talk and to your body's signals, you will find it easier to predict which commitments you are likely to keep ahead of time, so that you can choose to renegotiate or avoid making commitments that you won't be able to deliver on in the future.

- Taking time to learn what moves you to action will help stay inspired and in motion.
- You already have a unique personal success formula that has proven to be effective for you and you can intentionally apply it to the future situations.
- As a bonus you learned about the importance of organizing yourself for achieving the results that you want instead of focusing on managing time and tasks.

Suggested Next Steps and Exercises

- Explore your own relationship with commitments. What does commitment mean to you?
- Reflect on which commitments you keep and which ones you don't and how to develop the attunement to knowing right before you make a commitment if you intend to keep it.
- Reflect on what moves you to action. Write it down and use it intentionally to see if it still works in other situations. If yes, use it.
- Write down several stories of your own success and identify the common threads. Write out your own success formula, and test it out to other situations. Keep modifying and adjusting until it becomes the most effective.

* * *

You have covered so much already! I encourage you to take some time to really digest the material in this chapter. Once you are ready, I will see you in the next chapter, where you will explore deeper tools and practices for working with your energy to keep moving forward.

Chapter 7:

Receive Maximum Return on Your Energy Investments

"Energy and persistence conquer all things."
— BENJAMIN FRANKLIN

Intro to Energy Flow

In this chapter, I will go deeper into the subject that comes up with every single client that I have ever worked with – managing energy. Most people who come for coaching mention a goal of wanting to have more energy. It sounds simple and a common sentiment as people often are looking for ways to get more energy. However, what I have learned from the years of teaching and coaching, just like with money, it is a lot more useful to look at both the inflows and outflows of energy; in other words, it is a lot more effective to look at management of energy flows instead of just increasing how much you have coming in.

I will be sharing the top tools that I use with clients and myself for cultivating a more intentional and effective way of working and using the energy.

Most of you will intuitively sense that any action requires energy. Physicists have created formulas for calculating energy required to move something into action. I remember in a physics class, my teacher lectured on how much more energy is required for an object to be moved versus staying motion. It is intuitive. Just imagine trying to push a heavy boulder to roll, how much energy it would require. And now imagine a boulder rolling already with the velocity that has already been built. It would be a lot easier to maintain its speed with relatively little effort. That is the power of momentum.

In my observation, energy levels and energy flows serve as a mirror of how a client is doing inside and outside. Notice how when you are inspired and driven by a strong sense of purpose you seem to have an inflow of energy. The same goes for when you fall in love or get really angry at someone or something. Notice how these inflows of energy often happen fast and almost involuntarily but seem to be directly linked to the feeling state. Or notice what happens to your energy level when a loved one needs urgent help. Newspapers and blogs are full of stories of mothers demonstrating unprecedented levels of energy and physical strength when their child's life is in danger. Yes, there are a lot of chemical reactions happening in the mother's brain in these moments for energy to increase so rapidly in those situations. However, I am not as interested in the brain chemistry as I am in sharing an observation on how levels of energy get influenced by a vast number of both external and internal factors. My invitation is to bring more awareness to how your energy flows so that it is easier to work with it.

On a slightly different but related note, notice how energy needs to be used, in order to be replenished regularly. Just like a muscle that is unutilized, if energy has nowhere to go on a regular basis, the flow may quickly decrease. I see it as the body's natural way of rebalancing the energy system to function the most effectively. If it didn't, have you ever had an experience of having so much energy you didn't know how to use it and you were bursting? Do you remember how uncomfortable it may have felt? Where did that energy go? Imagine if you had to experience these overwhelming levels of energy and not being able to handle it on a daily basis. That would be a disaster. At the same time, have you ever had the opposite situation, when you find yourself barely having enough energy to go through the tasks of the day? I hear the latter one much more frequently. And yet, it is a similar example of lack of a healthy energy flow.

If you are like most of my clients, you may find yourself struggling with either inconsistent or insufficient flow of energy to show up fully for your goals and to enjoy your life as deeply as you would like. Or you may have big outbursts of energy that for some reason often may end in a crash. In the small chance that you are one of the lucky few who has a strong grasp on your energy flow and is satisfied with the way your energy levels are on a regular basis, you are welcome to skip this chapter.

Otherwise, I invite you to be patient with yourself and give yourself permission to take your time as you test out and apply the following concepts and practices. As you can see, the subject of learning how to work with energy flow involves many moving parts and yet it is crucial to sustainable success. I promise that mastering the skill of working with your energy flow will serve you in all areas of your life and especially in choosing and moving forward with your career.

Identify Your Current Energy Investments

The first tool in energy management that I introduce is identifying all the areas where a client is investing energy. This could be incredibly eye-opening. I invite a client to first identify big projects, intentional investments of energy such as her job; her relationship with her spouse, or kids, or friends; and hobbies. We then proceed to less conscious projects that still are pulling on the client's energy daily, and we identify any projects that a client has started that she has not finished. It could be projects around the house, ideas for vacations, mail that is not opened, and so on. Then we go deeper and look at any agreements the client has made that she didn't keep. Then we look at any investments into maintaining past trauma or worrying about the future. Every thought, feeling and every decision requires energy. For example, if the client has some unprocessed grief from a previous relationship, in order to maintain the feeling of grief active, she literally has to invest some of her energy on a daily basis, which is why letting go of old hurts could feel reenergizing.

I remember studying lectures by Caroline Myss on energy anatomy and energy flows. I loved how she spoke of energy management similar to managing money. Every thought, every judgment, every incident that gets you upset and worried – all of it requires energy investments. Most of us are investing so much of our energy in the past or the future that we barely have any left to be fully in the present, and then we wonder why we are so exhausted by midmorning. And this is also why, when someone goes through a big healing experience when they let go of something in the past, forgive something or someone, they often feel lighter and have more energy available to them on a regular basis afterward.

Of course, you cannot expect yourself to be perfect and I don't recommend becoming obsessive about closing all the open loops; however, there could be a lot of value in identifying the biggest leaks of energy and closing those. Think of each item as a separate credit card. You want to identify the ones with the highest interest rate and hopefully pay off and close those first. Same here. Sometimes, it could be as easy as declaring a project complete or renegotiating a commitment to someone or saying "no" to a project. And sometimes it could require more work, especially when you are dealing with grievances or trauma from the past. Working with a skilled and compassionate therapist or a trained coach could be very supportive. Later, in Chapter 9, I will share many tools for cleaning up your inner accounts. However, the first step that I do with clients who want to experience more energy is to invite them to identify and write down their "open loops" and all the places/thoughts/projects that they are aware of where they are currently investing their energy.

Once the clients are aware of the open loops that are depleting their energy, they can begin the process of intentionally closing the ones that they no longer want to keep open. I will be honest with you, this process can take some time, so I don't encourage clients to wait to take action until they are done. This is more of a long-term project and a practice that is very supportive to begin cultivating not just for the purpose of moving forward in your career but also for the purpose of being able to show up consistently and enjoying success in all areas of your life.

Return on Your Energy Investments (ROI on Energy)

Let's continue the theme of looking at managing energy as making investments and evaluating the return on these investments. When I was teaching finance, we often looked at ROI, return on investment. There are many ways to evaluate ROI, but the basic idea is to see how much more of value (in this case, energy) you get back in exchange for the original investment of energy.

 TIP: One way to look at ROI on Energy is to use the following formula: ROI = what you get (and what it means to you) – your investment of energy.

For example, one woman that I have been supporting has shared that she spent two to three hours every day either talking to or seeing a new man. She was investing even more energy as she was often thinking about him and their conversations. However, when I asked her about the return on her energy investments, she shared that she often felt less energized after their conversations. She was surprised to recognize that she was choosing to make these depleting energy investments. She looked deeper and she saw that she wanted to have a deeper connection with this man, and in some ways, she was hoping that spending time would bring them closer and build a deeper foundation. So she was looking at these energy investments as what accountants refer to as capital spending (i.e., building an asset or something she was hoping she would later be able to rely on). There is a lot of value in investing energy in building long-lasting relationships, but in my experience, you want to be clear and at least aware of ROI on your energy investments. For this woman, she chose to adjust how she spent time with this man. She decreased the amount of physical time and has done the inner work to shift her focus. She set healthier boundaries, so that she felt uplifted and nurtured. As a result, her ROI increased, as did her energy levels and curiously her relationship with the man improved as well.

Let me share another example from my own life. My first job out of college was an analyst position at a top investment bank. The required investment of energy was very high. I worked eighty to one hundred-hour weeks in a very high-pressure environment. I was making over $100,000 a year. I was also learning a lot and growing fast as a finance practitioner and in my life skills, as I was participating in meetings, dealing with high-pressure situations, and communicating with many stressed-out people all the same time. The first year, the return on my energy investment was high for me because there was a lot of value in the learning part. The second year, as I am getting more tired and the learning curve became more flat, even though the compensation increased, it wasn't enough to offset the decrease in the value of what I received (the value of learning), and I was ready for a shift.

I was very happy with my time at the bank by the time I left, because I still felt like I had an overall positive ROI. That said, I also know a lot of people who overstay at jobs when ROI turns negative leading to burnout and outbursts with much more devastating outcomes. So there is a lot of value in learning how to assess and work with your energy investments very intentionally.

Increase the Inflow of Energy

Now that I have opened the conversation discussing energy outflows and ROI, let's talk more about the inflows. Most people who come into my practice mention that they want to have more energy. Personally I often receive feedback that I am "naturally" a very high-energy person. I always smile and say thank you. I do function on a very high level of energy most of the time, but it is not a secret, and I don't consider myself to be special in any way or wired any differently. For me, I have been doing a lot of working on being intentional with how I spend my energy, and I am also continuously working on increasing my capacity to receive energy, to allow more energy to flow into my system.

If this sounds a little too conceptual, let me explain.

The first law of thermodynamics states that energy cannot be created or destroyed, it can only change form. What that means for you is that energy is everywhere and you choose how much energy you intake into your system. Some of that energy comes in from food and drinks. Nutritionists have been talking about the importance of the "right" calories for years, and there are numerous resources that you can look up for guidance with this. However, as a coach I notice that there are so many other areas to look to increase the capacity to intake and function on more energy. You can think of your capacity for how much energy you can receive and allow to pass through as voltage on a light bulb. Let's say I am used to functioning as a 60-watt light bulb, but I have this vision for a new business that will require me to shine more brightly so I can light up a bigger space, which will, in turn, require me to function at 150 watts. If I just "plug in" and let that much current run through my metaphorical light bulb, I will burn out very quickly. However, as a human, since my set points are adjustable, I can stretch and expand my ability to hold and function on higher and higher levels of energy. The key is to do it intentionally, gently, and consistently, in order to not to fry my circuits too quickly. And that is my intention for this section, to share some tools that I use with clients and myself to increase the capacity for higher energy inflow so that it's aligned with and supports the energy requirements of your Sacred YES vision.

One of the first areas that I invite the clients to analyze is their relationship with receiving and their capacity to receive. Before I even bring this up, I watch to see how the client responds to compliments or acknowledgments. Can the client gracefully receive opportunities, praise, money, or even a hug? These may sound unrelated, but in my experience, clients' openness to receive is one of the key factors to functioning on a higher level of energy. Let's be honest, not a single human on this planet creates energy. As the thermodynamics law states, energy can only change form. So for you to intake more energy, you need to have a system that is equipped to receive more.

Another metaphor: Let's say I want to get a drink of water and I go to the sink. I turn the knob, but I do not have a cup, or let's say my cup is tiny, cracked, and has holes in it. Imagine how frustrating it will be to drink from it. So instead of calling the plumber requesting to increase the water pressure in the sink, I suggest to get a bigger cup that you can use.

So the question becomes, how do you do that? How can you increase your capacity to receive and function at a higher level of energy voltage?

These are some of the practices that I have seen clients use very effectively to increase their capacity for feeling good on a more consistent basis and as a result for developing their ability to function at a higher level of energy. I invite you to reference this list for ideas and make up your own. The key ingredients are that the practice that you choose makes you feel uplifted, expansive, and connected to something bigger than you.

- Gratitude practice
- Saying "yes" and "thank you" to offer support, compliments, and similar

- Requesting support and being willing to receive with gratitude
- Spiritual practices/prayer
- Meditation/mindfulness practices
- Self-care – taking care of the body, such as getting a massage or going to spa, and scheduling and prioritizing fun and relaxing time with loved ones
- Saying and receiving the words "I love you"
- Giving and receiving hugs
- Calling a friend to both give and to receive support
- Volunteering, doing service work that is heartfelt and meaningful to the client
- Donating time, money, creativity, and other resources to projects you love and deeply care about
- Spending time with nature
- Spending time with music and art that you love
- Reading books by authors that fill you up with love and inspiration
- Listening to inspiration talks, videos and sharing those with others

You may have noticed how this list naturally includes both giving as well as receiving. In my experience, we cannot practice one without the other. I do want to make a note. I observed that some clients come in with a strong belief that giving is better than receiving. If that resonates for you, I invite you to look at that gently and work with this belief. You may even want to pause and flip to Chapter 9, which shares tools for aligning your mind and emotions for additional tips on how to work with limiting beliefs.

In my observation, giving and receiving is like breathing. I often ask a client, who is convinced that giving is better, to choose between inhaling or exhaling and offer a hypothetical situation where she can only choose one and do that for the rest of her life. Of course, it sounds ridiculous as one needs to do both to breathe. Giving and receiving is like that. If you slow down and look, giving and receiving go together everywhere. In nature there are organic laws of giving and receiving that are at the root of all cycles. As smart as our minds are, we are still a part of the natural world with its beautiful cycles and giving and receiving is a cycle that is one of the most basic. I invite you to embrace it and to enjoy all of it.

Once the clients begin to work with restoring a very healthy and natural cycle of giving and receiving for themselves, they not only notice an effortless balance that seems to come in all areas of their lives but also that they seem to have more energy flowing through them on a daily basis. That is very natural byproduct because they are more willing to receive and they are most likely digesting the energy that they intake more effectively as well. It is a beautiful phenomenon.

Get to Know and Use Your Natural Rhythms

Now that we have talked about both managing inflows and outflows and increasing the capacity for your body to handle and work on a higher voltage, another supportive inquiry to make is to look at your natural rhythms of energy during the day, week, and seasons. We all have them; some are very regular, and some may be consistently irregular. That is also a pattern. Whatever it is, it could be valuable to note.

For example, I have a client who is very energized in the mornings, but she is very depleted after 4:00 p.m. I have another client who takes about three hours to fully wake up but she thrives in the evenings and at night, which is when she creates her best work. I have another client who loves having a very regular schedule. She is a writer, and she works on her writing for an hour and a half every morning, Monday through Thursday. It works for her. I have another client who panics if I even mention something like a regular writing practice, but she is brilliant and bursting with creativity. We are all different, and there is value to begin to notice and adjust your schedule to work with your natural energy flows instead of trying to fit yourself into a box. All that said, sometimes you will find that having a regular routine will adjust your energy flows toward more consistency. I invite you to experiment and find out for yourself the best path for you.

Save Energy by Reducing Decision-Making Needs

This brings us to another point that I want to make here around routines and decision-making. In my experience, every decision requires energy to make. If it is a big decision it may require a lot of mental, emotional, and sometimes physical energy. Basically, it will require an energy investment. This is why when you have a habit or a routine, where you take decision-making out of the picture and choose to show up regardless of how you feel, simply because you have made a commitment, you may notice that you have more energy available for other activities in the day. This is so powerful because you no longer need to exercise extra energy on making that particular decision every time. Of course, it may take time to build a routine as there might be resistance at the beginning, which will require energy to dissolve. However, once the routine is set, it usually requires relatively little energy to maintain, which frees up a lot of energy for other projects and activities. This is why having routines and creating supportive systems can be so powerful. The key, of course, is to create routines that will be in alignment with what you want to create that honor you and your vision for your life.

Speaking of building routines for your life. One exercise that I use often with both business owners and professionals is asking them to reflect on what it would look like and feel like for them to show up fully in their work. Clients talk about being present, prepared, and engaged in certain types of activities. Once the client is clear about what that would look like, the next exercise is to evaluate if any of those could be made into routines and practices, so to incorporate into his or her life at the minimum energy investment need. It takes a bit of time to incorporate, but the results are always increased levels of available energy, a much higher level of joy and work satisfaction, and much greater effectiveness and success as clients measure it.

One of my friends and a fellow author who used to be a celebrity physical trainer for several decades mentioned that the clients who were the most successful were the most consistent. Consistency is more effective in the long run than sporadic intensity. This is not to negate those of you who like to burst into some of your projects. I am definitely one of those people who have slightly more irregular flow and to be honest I love it; however, I am still using the practices of consistency in showing up for my routines and I am consistently committed to my goals regardless of where my level of energy is for the day.

That brings me to one more tool that I want to share in this chapter that will greatly increase your effectiveness in energy utilization.

Dynamic Goal Setting for Maximum Energy Utilization

Most of my clients who come in are very motivated and ambitious. They often pick big goals and dive in. However, most fail at reaching all of their weekly goals at least at a certain point. What I notice is that most clients pick weekly goals in a linear way – that is, they assume that they will have the same level of energy (high) every day and should be able to produce at the same capacity (high) every day. When they inevitably hit the natural ups and downs in energy levels they stumble on meeting their goals, and then they start judging themselves for that, which depletes energy even further until they slow down and look more closely.

 TIP: Identify your goals and action steps and then sort your action steps based on how much energy they will roughly require. For example, you can sort your action steps by high/medium/low energy investment required. Or I like even simpler – high versus low energy required. You may find your own way to break the action steps. The key is to have flexibility in options for action steps so that you can keep moving forward regardless of how you are feeling energetically on any particular day.

Let me give you an example, I was working with a coach who supported me with writing this book. When I came down to the writing stage, some days I produced a lot and other days the writing wouldn't flow. So instead of forcing writing, I had other relevant projects that I engaged in, such as watching the corresponding training videos, reflecting, collecting research, and similar. This way, I kept staying productive while honoring the energy level of my body. I often invite clients to do the same with their projects. The key here is to become aware of where you are energetically and to accept it without judging so that you can choose the most productive activity.

The clients who master this level of intentional prioritization tend to flourish. And now I invite you to play with these tools as you move into action toward your Sacred YES vision!

Chapter Highlights

- Managing energy is about managing both the inflows and outflows.
- It is important to become aware of the ROI (return on investment) for your energy and to be intentional with projects, thoughts, and relationships you choose to invest your energy into.
- Some energy investments can become leaks, such as obsessing over something, having regret about the past, worrying about the future, making judgments,

and possessing negative thoughts or similar. Beginning to withdraw from these and similar activities will free up a lot of energy for other activities.

- You can increase your capacity for working with more energy by focusing on expanding your willingness to receive.
- Giving and receiving is a part of a natural cycle that is a foundation for all cycles.
- It can be fun and very useful to begin to get to know your own natural flow of energy more intimately and incorporate your observations into the planning process.
- Every decision requires energy, so building supportive routines and habits can free up a lot of energy for other activities.
- When identifying next steps for your vision, it could be useful to break up steps by the levels of energy required to execute them, so that you always have something you can do to stay effective and productive while honoring your natural flow of energy.

Suggested Next Steps and Exercises

- Write down your current energy investments. Think about all areas of your life, incomplete projects, relationships, conversations, books, thought patterns, dreams, obligations, and commitments. When complete, circle the most important ones and analyze their ROI. Do you feel recharged by these projects or do you feel depleted? If depleted, consider renegotiating them or completing.

- Reflect on your relationship with giving and receiving and consider engaging in some practices that facilitate deeper openness to receive from the list in the chapter.
- Reflect on your natural flow of energy during a day/week. How can you honor your energy flow and still schedule your projects for maximum results?
- Review your visions and analyze what kind of routines and systems could be supportive to prevent wasting energy on making similar decisions on a daily or frequent basis. Begin incorporating these systems and habits into your life.

Chapter 8:

Wire Resistance to Work for You

"What you resist not only persists,
but will grow in size."
— CARL JUNG

"In the middle of every difficulty lies opportunity."
— ALBERT EINSTEIN

Resistance

If you are reading at this point and have been incorporating the exercises and action steps, you are probably noticing how much resistance may have come up. Usually clients begin to feel resistance as soon as they show up and say "yes," but the resistance often reveals itself differently to everyone, and in my experience, clients who have learned how to work with dissolving their resistance along the way have enjoyed a much smoother journey than those who did not.

There is a lot of misunderstanding about what resistance represents. I want to support you with getting to know your own version of resistance more intimately and begin to create practices for dissolving it as well as using it as fuel to keep yourself progressing toward your desired professional expression.

Get to Know Your Set Points (i.e., Inner Thermostat)

When I have a new client come in who has never done any coaching, I often go over the concept of a "set point." Most clients are familiar with a similar concept of "comfort zone"; however, there is a lot more to be said here. In my experience, and there are lot of teachers and coaches who share this, you naturally create set points for pretty much anything in your lives. You can think of that as your state of equilibrium. Just like for most human bodies, the body will naturally be around 98.6 degrees Fahrenheit. It works the same for all kinds of feeling states and other areas of your life. For example, you will have a set point for how good you allow yourself to feel at work, for your level of happiness, for how much money you make and keep, for how much love you allow yourself to receive and on and on you go.

I realize it is a big blank statement to make, but I invite you to reflect on it. Have you noticed that even if something very traumatic happens, after a few hours or days you find yourself in a similar state of mood/mind that you had before the event? And the same often happens for something incredibly joyous coming in? This phenomenon has been observed and rigorously studied too. For example, in one of the many studies of lottery winners, it has been observed over and over again that most lottery winners are at the same place financially as they were before the winning within three to four years. The same goes for those who find themselves in a repeating dynamic in a relationship, effectively dating the "same" person over and over again. I have seen this with many clients I have worked with. Unless the clients choose to do the inner work that allows them to adjust the internal thermostat, their lives naturally will recalibrate to the "home frequency" or their natural set point. Coaching is all about supporting clients in shifting their set points toward a more desired place, which in turn makes it easier to move forward with their goals.

It may be a lot to take in, and if so, I invite you to take a break and reflect on your life and any set points you may be aware of. I invite you to look at multiple areas of your life and see what you notice.

Most clients who first begin becoming aware of their set points become discouraged, as they want their set point to be higher – for more joy, more love, more money, whatever it is that they want to create in their lives. However, set points are not good and bad and in many ways it is a very valuable tool that once understood, you can use to create a stronger foundation for your growth toward your goals.

The good news is that the set points work both ways. Let's say that I have a high set point for sharing, giving, and receiving love. Even if something happens and my partner or a friend is no longer there, I will naturally bounce back pretty quickly to my familiar set point, and I will organically find myself with another person to share my love with. You probably have at least one friend who always seems to "land on her feet." That is because her set point is high and is working well for her in that particular area.

Once they learn the concept of set points, the clients inquire about how to intentionally increase their set point to support them with their Sacred YES visions. I will share some of these tools later in this chapter. If you want more, you are welcome to also visit Chapter 9 for additional tips and practices in the area of the inner work.

True Meaning of Resistance

Let me share what I see happen often as clients begin to move toward their goals. Let's say a client wants to make more money in her business and serve greater audiences by selling her product online internationally. She will first experience a lot of enthusiasm because it is genuinely a heartfelt calling and then she will begin to stretch out of her comfort zone (i.e., her original set point) with some action steps. As she continues to do that, she will notice an increase in impact and revenue. Her set points for both her visibility and her openness to receiving revenue may get triggered. It is just like stretching a rubber band. At the beginning, it may feel like a slight tension, but as she keeps going, she will begin to experience more and more tension. This tension that she is feeling as she is stretching an "inner rubber band" is resistance. I imagine most of you have had an experience of what that feels like.

So one of the first things that I share with my clients is that feeling resistance is great. And I say that with sincere compassionate and humility. Here is why resistance is great. It is a clue that you are stretching yourself past the familiar set point. By the way, you will feel resistance regardless of the direction in which you are stretching. So if you are hitting resistance and you are moving in the direction that you want, know that you have an opportunity to not only dissolve the resistance so that you can continue to move forward, but to also move the entire set point upward, so that from then on, your entire set point in this area will be in a more desirable state. How exciting is that!?!

I realize it is all very conceptual so I will share more specific tools and examples as we go forward. Meanwhile, one key takeaway from here is that the feeling of resistance is completely normal and 100 percent guaranteed as you grow and move toward your goals. Learning how to work with resistance often becomes a key factor for determining if a person goes back to the original state defeated or if the inner set points get moved to a new equilibrium, which in turn helps achieving the goals.

Identify Your Flavor of Resistance

What does it mean to identify your own flavor of resistance? Over the years, I found it very supportive to identify how resistance shows up for each individual person. These insights become extremely valuable for recognizing resistance for what it is instead of being distracted or stopped by it.

Metaphorically speaking, when you are in a resistant state, it is like getting your car windshield completely fogged up. You literally cannot see. So it becomes dangerous and very ineffective to continue driving fast or sometimes at all. However, instead of using the appearance of resistance as a sign that you are not meant to do this, I invite you to use resistance as a clue that you are basically being stretched past a familiar set point, similar to shivering when the body is cold or sweating when the body is hot. You can work with it to move yourself forward. Using the car analogy, learning the clues for recognizing when you are in resistance, you can stop the car and focus on defogging your windshield before driving again. By mastering the tools of working with resistance, you will get to your destination much faster and the journey is likely to be smoother and more pleasant.

One exercise that I use often with clients and groups is to list different ways that they are aware that resistance shows up. If nothing comes to mind, I invite them to reflect on a situation when they were going for something that they wanted but was out of their comfort zone and share what happened both on the outside and on the inside during that process. Here are some of the most common examples that I hear. This list is by no means exclusive, as resistance has an unlimited number of flavors.

- Binge watching TV or Netflix
- Focusing on family drama

- Focusing on drama with a romantic partner/spouse
- Lots of attention and activity with sex/dating that requires energy
- Something happens in the client's personal life that is "really important" and needs attention ASAP
- Telling herself this is stupid and will never work, so she should stop now
- Telling herself she is worthless and not talented enough
- Telling herself that she cannot depend on others or trust anyone else but herself
- Telling herself that it is too late and she will never "make it"
- Telling herself that even though a process/program worked for others, it will never work for her because she is special in a way that is messed up
- Becoming completely bored with the original project/dream
- Getting depressed
- Experiencing an increased need for sleep
- Not being able to sleep from anxiety
- Getting deeply interested in a subject that is completely different
- Numbing activities like TV, drinking wine, smoking, complaining, and venting with friends, distracting with something silly
- Feeling overwhelmed

Some of these are behavioral, and some are more internal trains of thought. I do like to make a disclosure that not all of these necessarily always demonstrate a sign of resistance. For example, I may enjoy watching a TV show because I find it inspiring, and it has nothing to do with numbing or resisting my project. Or I may enjoy dating someone new and special that I'm excited about. What we are looking for at this stage is the behavioral patterns and thought patterns that seem to show up on autopilot when we feel uncomfortable.

Let me give you an example. I had a client who came in because she wanted to generate more revenue with her business, which required a lot of connecting and follow through. She came in full of enthusiasm and incredible presence. As she began to take action, she started sharing how much her family needed her attention all of a sudden. Her daughter needed her, then her son, then her husband, then something happened at her church that required her energy and focus, so she kept being pulled by all these "emergencies." It was a very powerful experience when she slowed down and began to realize that these "emergencies" were a sign of resistance that got activated as she began to stretch past her set point of how much success and how much money she was comfortable receiving in her business. She began to actively use the tools that I share and the "emergencies" slowly stopped as she freed up her energy and focus to devote to her business and her clients.

So step number one is to recognize when we are in resistance and to acknowledge it for what it is without making it wrong. In many ways, I would invite you to appreciate the resistance for showing up as you now have a clear clue that you are growing and you can use the energy of resistance to propel you forward even faster. That is the next step.

The question that clients usually have at this point is what to do once they are aware of resistance being present.

I want to share with you some of the tools that I have been personally using for many years and that many of my clients have applied very successfully.

There are three major approaches for working with resistance; the first two are widely used, and the third one may come as a surprise to some of you. The first approach is to elevate a particular set point to a higher level. I call this approach increasing the base-line temperature. We will talk about various ways we can do that. The second approach for dissolving resistance is to gently decrease the pull of the "inner rubber band." And then, there is a third way that may not be as widely known or intuitive, which takes the creative power of resistance and redirects it to move you forward toward your goals.

Shift Set Points to Higher Levels by Increasing Home Frequency

Similar to set points for various areas of your life, you will have a set point for how you tend to feel, I call it a home frequency. Some people refer to this as being an optimist or a pessimist, a generally happy person or a generally resentful person, or any other feeling state that is the most predominant.

In the context of a coaching conversation, executive coach and author of over thirty books, Steve Chandler calls these feeling states (home frequency and frequency scale) listed together a "ladder of consciousness." David Hawkins, a world-renowned psychiatrist, refers to various levels of feeling states as a consciousness scale. The idea is simple. Each thought and feeling state has a defined frequency that can be measured. You can easily tell the difference in feeling joy, happiness, sadness, anger, or resentment. Most likely you don't need a big scientific experiment to recognize the different feeling states and how they impact your productivity and experience of creativity.

For moving forward toward your vision and goals, one approach that I call the "top to bottom" approach is to apply tools to intentionally improve how you are feeling. This practice alone will increase the level of your focus, efficiency, and enjoyment of the process of reaching your Sacred YES vision.

Let's say my resistance shows up in me feeling lethargic, bored, and even slightly demotivated/depressed. Knowing this, I can choose to proactively engage in activities that make me feel good such as volunteering, yoga or dance, spending time in nature, or anything else that will move and elevate how I feel. I can also engage in a regular gratitude practice before I even get out of bed so that I train myself to keep vibrating at a higher frequency.

I remember when I first left my training job and was shifting into running my own business, I made a commitment to once a week volunteer at "School on Wheels" on Skid Row in downtown Los Angeles. I was working with kids whose families were homeless. What was ironic to me is that I originally thought that I was going to be the one who was giving and serving the kids. What I learned very humbly is how much I have received from that experience and how elevated, empowered, moved, and inspired I felt every time I came home and how much more energized I was to focus on what I wanted to create in my life. The weekly visits kept me grounded and grateful and helped redirect a lot of resistance in a way that was very surprising and effortless. I still devote a significant amount of time to volunteering and highly recommend finding a project of service for everyone who finds himself or herself demotivated or stuck. If you choose to look for a volunteer project, I recommend finding something that you will feel is close to your heart with people or animals and preferably something that is not related to your regular work, so that there is extra room for surprising discoveries.

Shift Set Points to Higher Levels by Appreciating Resistance

If you allow yourself to truly take some time to deeply appreciate resistance showing up, something very magical happens. The power that was used to prevent you from moving forward is now becoming available for you to use to move further along even faster.

For example, as I was writing this book, I hit a lot of roadblocks, the most recent one when I was planning to write this chapter. I had set aside time and shut off all electronics, and as I entered my office space with a desk right next to a balcony and my favorite tree, I saw in terror that there was a man on the tree cutting its lush branches that used to be a meeting place for birds and squirrels and my favorite hummingbird. My beloved tree got cut down in the span of two hours right in front of my eyes. It was very unexpected, and I cried. I even temporarily felt tempted to postpone writing the book, as I felt naked and exposed with the window and a balcony and no tree, birds, or squirrels that I used to love watching every morning.

Thankfully, I was reflecting on resistance, and I saw that this was an unexpected way that resistance showed up in my life that day. I will be honest it was painful. But then I chose to practice appreciation for the pain and appreciation for resistance showing up the way that it did. As I did that I felt much sadness and sorrow move through my body, I was grieving the tree but I was also grieving the person that I was with that tree, the person who was still hiding slightly and I was very aware of the gift of the open space that was created and the gift of open sky and the gift of visibility and also clearer vision. As I sat with the appreciation, I also felt like I was letting go of the old way of being and writing and stepping into a more mature more grounded way that was definitely in alignment with my vision for the book and the vision to serve more deeply. I still feel sadness about the tree trunk being so naked outside of my window and at the same time I am feeling more clarity coming in and deeper resolution for showing up and doing what is necessary to serve as deeply as I can as a writer and as a coach. This is an example of using appreciation of what is, appreciation of resistance in whatever shape it shows up so that it can translate into something that I could use to move forward.

Appreciating the resistance also showed me what was deeply important to me – being near nature, watching wildlife, and having a garden. It supported me in moving forward with a more robust understanding of my entire vision for what I would like to cultivate more of in my life, both in my home environment and how I want to spend my time. These are all very valuable gifts, and I am gratefully collecting them. Appreciating resistance is what allowed me to receive them while continuing to move forward towards my Sacred YES vision of writing this book.

I am laughing now because during the editing stage of this exact chapter, I noticed that I had more resistance show up. This time, the entire street block where I live went out of power for over twenty-four hours, so I spent the night as I was editing this chapter at my friend's house. I had also met an exciting new man earlier that day, so I found myself the evening that I was turning in the edits being pulled between editing and wanting to talk to my friend about the new man and showing her the pictures of his very cute cat. As fun and silly as it was, I recognized quickly that it was all resistance, and I appreciated it for what it was. Once I did, the focus and inspiration came and editing moved forward gracefully.

I am sharing these stories with an invitation of humility and humor, to hopefully support you with shifting how you view resistance from now on and maybe even have fun with it!

Shift Set Points to Higher Levels by Using Visioning Tools

Another tool to support shifting your set points is doing visioning work. Working with affirmations, vision boards, intentions, and prayers has proven to be very effective for not only focusing our mind in getting more clear on our goals but also in shifting our set point in the corresponding areas of our lives, as we literally retrain our minds and our bodies to be more familiar with what we want to create.

A similar tool would be the practice of "trying on your vision for size" that we covered in Chapter 5, and also connecting with the Future Self. All of these exercises serve two key purposes, gaining more clarity and shifting the corresponding set points in addition to increasing the home frequency as you feel more joyful and excited about your vision.

Shift Set Points to Higher Levels by Taking Bold Action

One last tool that I want to mention here is taking BOLD action. I don't offer it to all clients, but for those who are ready, this can be very powerful and fun. One way that I often recommend to approach working with bold action is to make a game out of it. The key here is that you intentionally choose to take action that you know will trigger you and will 100 percent take you out of your comfort zone. And, regardless, you choose to take the action. Then by taking it and surviving (as you most likely will) you are literally reprogramming your brain to no longer see that particular action or similar action as dangerous. The part of the brain that is responsible for triggered fear mode (amygdala) does not get activated as much in the future and your set point shifts organically in that particular area.

For example, I have a client who is growing her coaching practice. She enrolled a few clients quickly but then hit a plateau for two months and was getting discouraged. Knowing her fiery nature, I invited her to take some bold actions of reaching out to nonprofit organizations in the area, which was relevant to the type of coaching that she did, and she lit up. Over the next several weeks, she did just that, and she was transformed. Not only did her practice grow, but she also had a lot of fun and reclaimed her authentic voice as a coach. She used all the built-up pressure of resistance and channeled it into a game of bold action. The key with bold action is to be willing to show up fully and not be attached to getting a specific outcome.

Here is another example of bold action shifting a set point. In my Toastmasters group, a fellow member was very afraid of public speaking. In fact, the first meeting that I had ever attended, she came out to give an impromptu speech and then she went completely blank and couldn't say a word for two minutes. We all clapped regardless at the end to acknowledge her. What is interesting is that after that experience she never felt blank again (at least to my knowledge) and kept showing up and giving talks. Her public speaking improved, but even more importantly, she no longer would freeze up in similar situations. For her, the bold action of showing up and being willing to be seen as she went blank and then continuing to keep showing up and giving talks, desensitized her to the fear of public speaking. Using our set points analogy, her set point for what she thought was possible for her around self-expression, and especially speaking in an unplanned situation, has shifted in a positive direction.

Reduce the Pull of Resistance by Writing and Burning

The second path to working with resistance is centered around relieving some of the pressure to prevent the amygdala (the fear center of the brain) from getting overly activated and to allow for the chosen action to continue. Using our rubber band metaphor, the focus here is on reducing the pull of the rubber band so that the band doesn't snap and we keep some mobility.

One tool that I personally use at least several times a week, and which I often recommend to clients, is writing and burning. For example, I had a client who came to me to identify how she wanted to grow in her career. As we began working together, she started having a lot of unexpected conflict with her boss who, according to my client, started acting flat-out abusive. As we dove deeper into the situation, my client had an "aha!" moment, that her boss's behavior was an opportunity for her own resistance to show up as she needed to find her voice as part of her growth process. So, this client had a lot of anger on a daily basis, that kept leaking her energy and distracting her from her bigger vision. One of the tools that I offered her and that she used almost daily for several months, was the practice of writing and burning, which was incredibly effective. The way that I recommend using it is with the intention of releasing any toxic buildup of energy, emotions, and thought patterns to relieve some of the pressure.

The steps for the writing and burning practice is to sit down in a private space, set the intention to clear as much negativity as possible, and to begin writing or scribbling whatever is present in the mind. The key is to get the energy out and to not reread what you wrote. I learned this tool when I was receiving my MA in spiritual psychology where my teachers also recommended lighting a candle before you engage in it. Once you finish writing, you want to take all the papers and burn them, shred them or flush them down the toilet. The intention is to release it completely. You may want to wash your hands afterward, too, to physically cleanse from the energy. It sounds like a very simple practice; however, in my experience it is still one of the most effective tools that I personally use to keep negativity and pressure from building up so that I can proceed through life and my projects with more joy and ease.

Reduce the Pull of Resistance by Doing Inner Work

As you may have noticed, resistance often shows up as a very strong feeling, such as anxiety, restlessness, or of being overwhelmed, or a depleting negative thinking spiral of self-criticism. The good news is that once resistance activates these feelings and thought patterns you can use tools in clearing them once and for all. This practice is so important that I chose to devote the entirety of Chapter 9 to going deeper into this area.

You are welcome to pause and reference that chapter if you have a lot of resistance coming up. In my experience as a coach, about 80 percent of resistance (could be more) is related to the inner work, so applying the practices for aligning the mind and emotions with your goals will most likely dramatically impact your journey as the resistance declines and you proceed forward more gracefully.

Reduce the Pull of Resistance by Giving Yourself a Break

Another way to relieve some of the pressure from resistance is to intentionally give yourself a break. For example, you may want to give yourself permission and actually organize a social gathering or go dancing or do something else that is very physical and positive to relieve the built-up energy in a way that you choose. Notice the key here is to be intentional versus letting the pressure of resistance escalate to the point that it bursts and you may be tempted to act out and regret later as you may unintentionally hurt your projects, your loved ones, or yourself.

Reduce the Pull of Resistance by Giving It Voice

There are many other tools. I will share one more and we will cover additional deeper ones in the next chapter. Many of my clients comment on being stuck. This is a type of resistance, and there are many tools for working with it. One is to give voice to stuck-ness and ask it to share what "it needs/ wants." If you are a writer, you can write about being stuck. If you are an artist you can do an art piece about being stuck. If you like to move and express yourself through the body, you can give yourself permission to move as stuck-ness. Stuck-ness is basically resistance to digesting something or resistance to accepting something that is coming through. So being with your stuck-ness, giving it voice, and room to be, is often all that it needs to begin moving again. Similar to this tool, you can try getting curious and sharing with a friend about your experience of stuck-ness from a place of curiosity, as if you are an investigative journalist interviewing stuck-ness. What is that all about? You get the idea.

Use Resistance to Speed Up Your Progress

In this step, I want to share an unexpected discovery that I have made over the years of working with clients and with my own journey with resistance. Remember our earlier analogy of stretching a rubber band? Well, you feel the pull of it, which is resistance. However, instead of simply focusing on dissolving it, it is even more effective if we take the energy that is now being stored in the stretched-out rubber band and use it to move ourselves forward even faster. How exciting would that be?! If you don't connect with what I am sharing, just take a rubber band, stretch it, and then let go; notice how much energy it has as you let go. The entire art of archery is designed based on this principle, and now I am inviting you to use it, use the resistance to propel you and your project forward.

The question is, how can we do that?

The first step is to recognize and to acknowledge that we are in resistance. This gives us awareness that we have energy that is currently being used against what we want, and then we want to simply redirect it so that it moves us forward.

The second step is to change the context for resistance as a trigger for call to action instead of a call to stop. This step is truly a life mastery in of itself. Given the constraints of a book, I will share some high-level concepts. And I invite you to consider this an invitation into a lifelong practice.

Since resistance shows up in many different shapes, different tools would be appropriate at different times to switch the direction and to harvest the energy of it. But the key is to preemptively explore creative solutions for redirecting energy that is being built up in resistance to free it and redirect it to move forward even faster.

Chapter Highlights

- You have invisible set points for everything from happiness and prosperity to how much love you allow yourself to receive.
- As you begin to move forward toward a goal, you move upward from your familiar set point and experience resistance.
- Resistance is a helpful clue and can be used to support you in moving forward even faster or, if left undetected and untreated, can pull you back to the original set point.
- Resistance can show up in many ways, and it is important to become familiar with how resistance shows up for you so that you can work with it proactively.
- Appreciating resistance can turn it from a roadblock into a stepping-stone.
- Elevating your state of consciousness via service, doing what you love, being in nature, and similar activities can help shift your set point as you grow.
- Getting curious about resistance and giving it voice could be a fun and effective tool for dissolving the resistance.

- Writing and burning is another powerful tool for releasing toxic built-up energy of resistance.
- Taking bold action or intentionally relieving the pressure with a physical activity or similar could be fun and very supportive to keep going.

Suggested Next Steps and Exercises

- Identify your own flavor of resistance and write it down. Make sure to reflect and include both the behavior/external ways that resistance shows up. What are your recurring thought patterns and things you begin telling yourself when resistance is full on for you?
- Proactively contemplate some emergency exit plans for what you will do when resistance hits – and have a list ready for action.
- Incorporate a daily practice of relieving toxic energy with a writing and burning practice or a form of a physical exercise or anything else that you can build into your calendar that is there to support you to avoid high pressure built up from resistance.
- If it seems fun, play a game of taking bold action. It is even more fun with a friend. Choose a timeline – a week or several weeks – and go for it. Be clear about your priority. Take bold action and find a way to reflect either via journaling or talking to a friend.

* * *

I recognize that this was a very loaded chapter. Resistance is not a fun topic for most people, and yet, as you can see, you can incorporate fun into how you work with it. If resistance has come up strong as you were going through the material, this is another good time to take a break from the reading and watch the supplemental master class on *How to Handle Fear Effectively*.

You can download it here: clearwaycoach.com/free

* * *

Now that you have identified why resistance has to show up, in the next chapter we will go deeper into the tools and practices for working with the resistance from the inside out as we talk about aligning our mind and emotions.

Chapter 9:

Align Your Thoughts and Emotions for Success

"There is nothing either good or bad
but thinking makes it so."
— WILLIAM SHAKESPEARE

"We cannot solve our problems with the same thinking
that we used when we created them."
—ALBERT EINSTEIN

The Inner Work: Alignment between Three "Selves"

If you have been following along and doing the core exercises,
you may have noticed that in order to stay clear and move

forward toward your Sacred YES vision, it is important to master working with the resistance and any feelings that come up, hence the importance of the inner work. I like to think of this process as a practice of cultivating a state of inner alignment between three "selves".

The first self many coaches and therapists refer to as the Heart, the Higher Self or the Inner Wisdom, basically the part that you have been connecting with that generated the Sacred YES vision. The second self is what most therapists refer to as the "ego" or "personality." This self is composed of your mind and your emotions. And the third self is our physical body. I like to place the body into a separate self bucket, because in my experience, the body has its own level of wisdom, which is separate from the mind/emotions and the Higher Self.

What happens typically when a client shows up and sets a clear vision with the Higher Self is that the body and the mind/emotions may or may not be on board. If a vision is a big stretch, it is more often than not that each self is likely to pull in slightly different directions.

For example, I can have an inspiration to get in shape for a marathon. I have my Sacred YES vision, so my heart is in! Then I notice that my body somehow still wants to eat cookies and feels cranky when I wake up at 5:00 a.m. to go on a morning run. And I also notice that my mind starts telling me that it is a stupid idea to run a marathon anyhow with all my work and life commitments. So if I don't address this misalignment it is very likely that I will stop very quickly. If I am extra stubborn, I can push through, but it is likely to be painful. The progress can unfold much more gracefully if I intentionally work on cultivating and maintaining the inner alignment between the three selves so that they all pull in the same direction.

So far we have been focusing on aligning the Higher Self and the body self with your vision. In this chapter I will be introducing tools for cultivating the inner alignment with the "personality self," which includes mind and emotions. Specifically I will elaborate on how you can support yourself with a four-step strategy to get yourself back on track when your mind spirals down and emotions go awry as you begin to take action.

However, before we jump into the four steps, let's identify where feelings come from and how the behavior patterns get created. I refer to this process as "taking ownership" of the "inner reality".

The Power of Taking Ownership

When a new client comes in, I often take out a marker and draw two diagrams, both of a loop of events, thoughts, feelings and behavior. The first one looks something like this:

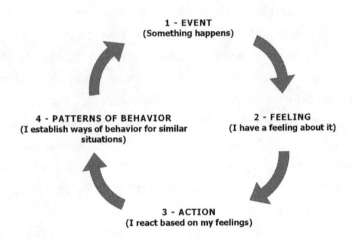

Everyone usually nods in agreement. Most new clients take the premise that an event leads to a feeling for granted as the only way to be. An event happens, let's say a boss yells at them; they feel triggered and get sad; they shut down, get upset and distracted and miss the deadline for a project later that day; the boss yells at them again; they feel even sadder and lose more self-confidence; and the loop continues. They make a conclusion that the boss is a jerk and either choose to suffer quietly, stay away, or eventually start looking for another job. There is technically nothing wrong here, but notice how disempowering the entire situation is for the person involved.

Unless you have done a lot of the inner work in therapy or coaching, or have been fortunate to grow up with very aware parents/guardians and teachers, most of you probably have not been taught to question that an event leads to a feeling. And notice, how, since you cannot control all of the events, this premise leads to a default conclusion that you are a *victim* of the event. And as a coach, I see how dangerous this is, because once you identify yourself as a victim in any way you have given up the power to make any positive change.

However, if you choose to slow down and really question the progression of each segment in the first loop, it is technically not accurate at all, or better said, it is not complete as this diagram misses a very imperative step! And that step takes place *after* the event and *before* the feeling. It happens in less than a second and it determines the rest of the loop progression and that is your *interpretation* of the event. In other words, what you make the event mean about the world and about yourself.

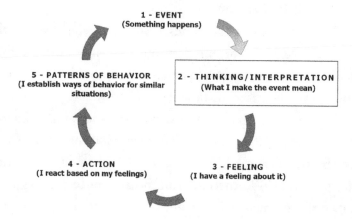

Notice, in this scenario, the loop progression does not depend on the *event* at all, but it depends fully on your *thinking* and the *interpretation* of the event. This is why many teachers, coaches and therapists focus on the mindset and on working with the clients' beliefs. I am not saying that you want to ignore the event itself or not have the goals; quite the contrary, I love supporting clients with setting and reaching goals. What I am offering here is *freedom in choosing how* you are moving along to those goals instead of feeling imprisoned and enslaved to any external events that may come up on your way to your goals, so you get to enjoy moving toward your goals faster and more gracefully. In my experience, it makes all the difference!

The key then becomes to learn how to build awareness, identify the interpretations that you are making, and actively choose the interpretations/beliefs that will support you with reaching your goals.

Step 1: Build Awareness

If you are new to the mindset work or if you have mostly only worked with the mindset and not emotions, the first step is to begin to develop a practice that would allow you to slow down the moment between the event and your feeling about the event and to notice the corresponding thinking or interpretation/conclusion that your mind makes. It is not easy by any means, and it is one of the highest ROI activities you will ever do in the long run, because once you begin to notice the moment when you make the interpretation, you put yourself in the position of power where you get to choose to keep the interpretation or to make another one. If you don't catch the interpretation and allow the feeling to define the action (or reaction in this case), what happens is the feeling will often generate similar thoughts and similar actions, so the loop often spirals down quickly. This is why if you have a "rough" morning, it is sometimes easy to spiral down and have a "rough" day at work. The sooner you catch yourself, the sooner you can course correct. So step one is building awareness of the moment when you make up a conclusion or a story about the event.

Some tools for building awareness are the mindfulness practices mentioned earlier in the book. That said, I have another tool that I personally use and often recommend to clients who want to go deeper, quicker. It is a journaling practice of being an observer of your thoughts and feelings and recording both very strong positive feelings and corresponding situations/interpretations that bring up the positive emotions as well as the negative feelings and the corresponding situations/interpretations that trigger the negative emotions. The key is to observe from the most neutral place that you can. It could be a fun exercise to capture the feelings as if you are conducting an experiment. It is also very eye-opening to review these entries later, let's say at the end of the month and identify any patterns. These patterns become very obvious hence, much easier to catch and reroute next time a similar situation comes up.

Step 2: Identify the Beliefs/Interpretations

The next tool that I often use with clients is to take any belief or interpretation and look at it as if you were to buy it at a store. How much value would you put on it? Would you want to buy it? If yes, how would you use it? How would it serve you? What is the price tag? In other words, what is this thought/interpretations costing you? Does it feel good in your body? If you get a sense that it is not really serving you, then consider "returning" it. I promise you there is an unlimited return policy on any thoughts and beliefs for all! Most likely it is a way of thinking that you have picked up from someone else, either a parental figure or culture or friends or colleagues.

The majority of limiting thoughts that I hear from clients are not very original. They may include:

- I am not good enough.
- I am unworthy.
- I need to be validated to have self-worth.
- I have to work hard for money.
- There is not enough money/resources/jobs/ opportunities/love for everyone.
- I have to compete to survive.
- I cannot do what I love and be prosperous.
- I have to choose between pursuing my dream and paying bills.
- It is too late for me to go for my dreams.
- I am too old/young/tall/short/etc. or not enough.
- I don't have enough time.
- I cannot be a good parent/family member and have a successful career.

None of these are supportive to creating the work that you love, and yet, it can be tempting to keep buying into them and continue using them and paying the high price with no value or very little value whatsoever. It is like buying an ugly outfit as a teenager to please your friends and then choosing to wear it every day for decades as an adult even though you could easily buy another outfit. What I am offering here is the idea that you are continuously choosing these "outfits" – which are your interpretations of the world, others, yourself – and that some of you may have been choosing by default and the default is usually not so great. So I invite you to begin upgrading your interpretations to what you actually want to use at this stage of your life.

100 Percent of Your Beliefs are True ... for You

Some clients get excited about this and others doubt and challenge me on the idea that they can choose their beliefs, listing evidence for why their core beliefs are "true." If you are feeling this way about your beliefs, I will 100 percent agree with you. In fact, I will go even a step further and say that 100 percent of all of your beliefs are true – for you. They have to be; otherwise, they wouldn't be your beliefs. Your mind simply cannot accept anything else into your system that is not true according to your beliefs. In a case of facing a contradicting event or a new belief, the mind will either have to reject and not accept the new input or let go of the old belief, which will now be proven wrong.

This principle is so important; if you take nothing else from this entire book but really integrate this principle into your mind and your way of living, you will be able to create a career and a life that is beyond anything you have ever dreamed of.

I just made a very bold statement that 100 percent of all of your beliefs are true for you. I will make a second bold statement – 100 percent of your beliefs will not be true for someone else. This is usually pretty obvious if you observe others. After working with so many students and clients over the years, I noticed that the combination of beliefs is as unique as a fingerprint; everyone seems to have a very special combo even if you have lots of similarities to someone else.

And you also probably have noticed that it is possible for someone to change their core beliefs. All of these observations lead to a conclusion that beliefs are not 100 percent true for everyone, which means there is no such thing as an absolute true "core belief" system, but the beliefs are more like programs that you choose to install on our "inner computers" to run your operating system. You need them to operate your mind/emotion system, but you can always choose to "upgrade" to a more effective set of beliefs. In my experience, that is one of the most effective acts you can do.

Let me explain what I mean. Let's say as an example, I grow up in a tough economic situation (which I did), so I am taught to believe that I have to work hard for money. I grow up, go to college, get a solid job in finance and begin earning money, but I am tired and working around the clock. If I keep this belief that I have to work hard for money, I will notice that I cannot receive a job or a business opportunity that generates money in an easy and fun way. It would be a contradiction for the mind and I would have to prove myself (i.e. my mind) as "wrong." The mind does NOT like to be proven wrong and will do anything to stay "right," even at a very hefty price tag. So if an opportunity to earn income doing something easy and fun comes along I most likely will not trust it, not recognize it, or sabotage it in some way. If I am aware enough from doing the inner work to catch the opportunity and the limiting belief, I may seize the opportunity, but then I will need to shift the underlying belief in order to keep it, or the gig will not last.

I used to love math when I was in high school. And I remember in a geometry class the teacher would invite us to use theorems (basically ideas) that were proven and accepted as true to be used to prove other theorems and problems that may or may not be true. In other words, I would use what I know to define what I don't know.

The same works for your beliefs; you use them as theorems, accepting them to be 100 percent true to define the rest of your life, what "input" from the outside world you choose to receive, which relationships, which events, which opportunities you say "yes" and "no" to. And these core beliefs are running until you choose to disprove them based on a life event or let them go intentionally.

The good news is just like with the set points, your beliefs can support you with what you want to create in your work, so the key is to not bash the system of beliefs but to learn how to use it to your advantage!

Step 3: Update Limiting Beliefs

Once you begin to identify your current interpretations and beliefs, you may find that some are working great for you and some you want to "upgrade." In that case, below are some questions that I often ask my clients to reflect on as they go through the process of updating their beliefs and interpretations.

What would you be feeling/doing *without* this belief/ interpretation? Notice how your body feels. Does it feel lighter or more expansive? If yes, that is a clue that the current belief is adding weight and constricting your life. Once you have made that connection, you can choose to explore alternative interpretations/beliefs around the subject.

Pick an interpretation that feels good in your body and find proof from life – two to three instances when that interpretation was "true." By finding "proof" of the new belief, you are "installing" the new software and allowing yourself to integrate the new "belief program."

If it resonates, I often have clients create an affirmation, a mantra, or a reminder that this is the new belief that they are choosing to use.

TIP: If you are new to affirmations, there is a lot of material out there. One of my favorites is still the work by Louise Hay. I highly recommend to look up her books online. Very briefly, a powerful affirmation is a positive statement of what you want to be true, in the present tense, with some energizers from positive feelings. For example, "I am enjoying deeply meaningful work and generous compensation!" Or "Money flows easily and gracefully into my life!"

Here is a quick example of a client who reset her beliefs. Let's say a client has a limiting interpretation that she cannot make sufficient income doing what she loves, so she stops herself from even trying to pursue her dreams. She becomes aware of her limiting belief and asks herself how she would feel if this belief was not operating. She notices that if she doesn't have this limiting belief "active" she feels lighter, more open to ideas, excited to try some of those ideas out, and more hopeful about her future prospects for her work. She goes deeper and realizes that she had been making an inner choice of staying in a victim position and feeling disempowered so that she didn't have to take any risks and her corresponding external choice had been spending her evenings watching Netflix or hanging out with friends complaining about her job and being stuck.

She identifies that she has other choices, such as changing her belief as well as beginning to take steps toward exploring her options. She goes into more specifics with interpretations and comes up with an alternative that affirms that "it is possible to create financial prosperity doing work that I love." She then writes down an instance when she made money doing something she loved as a teenager and then two other stories – one of her friend who is financially thriving in her business that she loves and another one of Oprah, who is her role model. Notice she didn't even need to find these "proofs" in her own life. The fun thing is, if an "interpretation" can be true for one person, it can also be true for you, if you *choose* it to be, as you are ultimately the one who is choosing which beliefs to "buy" and what value to place on them.

Going back to the client, now she is feeling even more excited and to help herself continue integrating her new interpretation, she writes down an affirmation to practice out loud in front of a mirror daily – "I am enjoying financial prosperity doing work that I love!" She also places a picture of Oprah and her friend who has a successful business and herself as a teenager with her first job that she loved and looks at those as she practices her affirmation. Very quickly she notices that she feels better and she is more open to ideas and has more energy, so the next time she gets an inspiration to speak up and share her idea with a new friend at a dinner party, the person gets excited and shares an opportunity and the client finds herself shifting into a new project and soon a new line of work very gracefully while having so much fun along the way!

One question that I am sure you have heard is this one – "Would you rather be right or happy?" It is a fantastic one to reflect on daily. If you find yourself being extra attached to proving a certain belief as "true," and it is not a belief that produces the desired outcome for you, you may find it valuable to remind yourself that you are choosing in this very moment to be right. And there is absolutely nothing wrong with that. It is wonderful and it may feel comforting, and you may also be paying a very high price tag. And you can always choose differently at any moment.

Some clients get a bit confused and concerned at this point, getting worried that if they stop trying to prove that they are "right," they will have no spine or stop fighting for what they believe in. In some ways, as a society we train ourselves to value judgment as a crucial component, a glue that holds a responsible citizen together. However, if you are willing to slow down and challenge even this perspective that you need to judge and be right, notice what happens when you judge.

You get angry or sad, your energy depletes, your brain stops generating ideas and you most likely get triggered and become emotionally reactive, which means that the blood flow shifted toward your reptilian brain or the emotional brain. In many ways, you are actually less capable of responding and enacting positive change when you are in this state of reactivity. Hence, by doing the inner work and clearing any judgments or limiting beliefs, not only will you feel better, but you will also naturally become a significantly more effective agent of positive change in this world! If you don't believe me, give it a try and see for yourself!

Practicing 100 Percent Engagement / 0 Percent Attachment

Before we move to the final step in our four-step process, I want to address a common misunderstanding that I see with the clients who want to use the affirmations and rewire their limiting beliefs, but who become resistant to the act of claiming what they want in order to avoid becoming too "attached" to the outcome. Or some other clients embrace claiming what they want but then they get deeply attached to the outcome, which actually often sabotages the progress or at least slows it down. So I want to share a few things.

One is an important difference between being attached to a specific outcome versus having a preference. The first one is driven by "lack" or fear that we don't have it, which leads to the idea, "I must have this outcome." The latter one is rooted in a place of freedom, "I prefer, I get to have an outcome, it is a game and that is my preference" and "I also know that I will be OK without it." Notice the difference.

There is another way to think about this that I love. I learned this one from one of my teachers at the University of Santa Monica, Dr. Mary Hulnick. She would often promote "100 percent engagement/participation and 0 percent attachment." Notice how the focus here is on being fully present and in action without allowing the outcome to define the action. In many ways, this way of approaching any project has always generated even better outcomes and opportunities for my clients than we originally could have imagined. It does take time to shift into this way of approaching projects and I highly encourage you to test it out for yourself.

All of these tools and practices are only as good as their applications, so I always invite clients to test them in their lives before they buy them. If they work and produce desired results, great! Otherwise, let them go.

Step 4: Process Feelings Effectively

Most clients who come in, and I certainly have been there myself, tend to avoid feeling negative feelings. It is completely understandable: they don't feel good. What I discovered as I worked with more clients was that most of them had a semiconscious belief that they could not handle a certain intensity of emotion and that they needed to protect themselves from strong feelings. As a result once the client would go past a certain set point, he would find a way to suppress and numb feelings. In many ways, the clients literally refused to digest feelings. Then what happened, just like when you eat something you cannot digest, was that the feelings would get stored in the body for many years, until the clients do a crazy cleanse (a.k.a. have an emotional meltdown or getting burned out) and everything would come out!

The good news is we don't have to wait to cleanse the emotions, and there are many gentle and effective tools for beginning to build your own mastery in digesting the emotions.

 TIP: David Hawkins has done an incredible level of work in this area. One of my favorite books on this subject is *Letting Go*, and I highly recommend it for a deeper dive into the topic.

Meanwhile, some tips that I often use myself and offer to my clients are the following. Once you become aware of a negative feeling, if you catch the point of thinking spiraling down, apply the first step of radical acceptance. Accept the fact that you have gotten triggered and are experiencing an upset emotion. Do your best to not judge it. It is OK! We are all human and this is a part of being human!

If you have time and space, give yourself a minute to feel the emotion in your body, focus on the sensation. According to Dr. David Hawkins, if you catch yourself early without letting thinking spiral down and just let the feeling flow through the body, it cannot stay more than twenty seconds. Feelings are just energy and they have to pass, unless you resist them. Resisting them gives them energy so they can refuel and stay in the body longer.

Another approach for releasing feelings is a practice of forgiveness. There are many ways to practice forgiveness. However, I want to share a slight twist on forgiveness. Most of you probably had an experience of a relief when you have let go and forgiven someone or yourself for a past incident. It can be such a powerful experience.

When I work with clients, I offer them to take forgiveness even further. Using the diagram from the beginning of this chapter that highlights how it is not the event but our interpretation of the event that leads to the feelings, you can "supercharge" the forgiveness practice, by going for the "root" and forgiving yourself for any limiting misinterpretations and beliefs you may have bought into.

In my experience, practicing forgiveness in this way is very powerful and releases a lot of stuck energy, which can then be used productively for moving the client's goals forward.

For example, let's say I have a speech to give and don't prepare much, so it doesn't go very well. I may have an interpretation that I "messed up" and that "I am not good enough" and that "I am a bad speaker." The corresponding feelings most likely will be feelings of sadness and low self-worth. If I go through the process outlined in this chapter and identify that the "root" of my sad feelings and low self-esteem was not the "poor speech" but my "interpretation," I can choose to apply the forgiveness practice for the interpretation. I could say something like, "I forgive myself for judging myself as a bad speaker," or "I forgive myself for buying into a misunderstanding that because of this one talk I am not good enough and can never be a good speaker." Notice

I am forgiving myself for the interpretations and not just the behavior. This is an important key so that I can free myself from the weight of the misidentifications that I am "not good enough," and I am much more likely to step up and deliver a more powerful talk with more confidence if I don't have the limiting belief operating.

 TIP: In my coaching practice, I utilize a lot of tools from my master's program in spiritual psychology at the University of Santa Monica. If you are curious to go deeper into the above forgiveness practice, I highly recommend reading *Remembering the Light Within* by Drs. Mary and Ron Hulnick. It covers a lot of similar tools in detail and is a fantastic resource.

Chapter Highlights

- Aligning three "selves" – the Higher Self, the mind/emotions "self," and the body "self" – is key to moving forward toward your goals most effectively.
- Your feelings and actions are heavily influenced by your *interpretation* of the events in your life. By changing the interpretation of the event and beliefs that define and drive your life, you get to choose what kind of life and experiences you get to create. You get to choose which interpretations/stories/beliefs you place value on and use in your life and you can change them at any time!

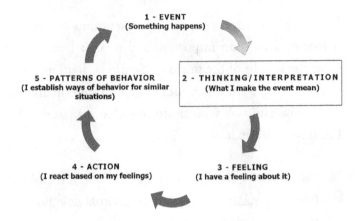

- **Step 1:** Build Awareness – Begin to notice the moment between the event and your feeling with the intention of capturing the interpretation of the event/belief that is operating.
- **Step 2:** Identify Limiting Interpretations/Beliefs – Once you capture the interpretation, evaluate if it feels expansive or constrictive, that is, how is it serving you? Does it produce the results that you desire?
- **Step 3:** Update Limiting Beliefs – Consciously go through the process of choosing into an alternative set of beliefs and find proof that the new belief is "true." Practice until the new belief is "installed," remembering that 100 percent of your beliefs are true – for you. And you are the one who chooses which beliefs are operating in your consciousness and can change them at any time!
- **Step 4:** Process Feelings Effectively – Applying the practice of forgiveness of the interpretation of events is one way to release negative emotions. Another

practice is allowing the feeling to flow through the body without resisting it as best as you can. According to the research by Dr. David Hawkins, if you don't resist a feeling and don't attach more thoughts to it, it can only stay in the body for about twenty seconds before it dissipates or gets refueled with resistance or another thought.

Suggested Next Steps and Exercises

- One way to apply the lessons in this chapter is to look at how well you are "digesting" your experiences, thoughts, and feelings. By digesting I mean accepting and processing. Indigestion of feelings or experiences leads to what most clients refer as "stuck-ness." Fears and limiting stories you may be telling yourself lead to indigestion. Acceptance of the situation without any judgments and willingness to embrace all feelings about it often dissolves stuck-ness very quickly. So a great exercise could be to reflect on the question: What is it that I have been unwilling to accept (i.e., digest) about this situation?

- Go through the exercise of identifying and challenging the thought/interpretation about an event/others/ yourself/life and choose an alternative one to incorporate.

- Practice accepting and being with your feelings and watch how long they can stay in your body without additional input of self-judgment.

- Practice forgiving not just other people or yourself but also your interpretation of what happened. For example, "I forgive myself for judging my boss as not fair when I didn't get a promotion." Or, "I forgive myself for judging myself as not good enough when I didn't get the promotion/a job offer."

* * *

We have covered a lot of material on how to work with the limiting beliefs/thinking and process emotions in this chapter. Take some time to play with the exercises to see which ones are the most effective for you. These will prepare you to receive the maximum value as we go for the gold in the next chapter to support you with removing any inner blocks on how much money you have been able to generate and enjoy.

How amazing will you allow your life to be?

Chapter 10:

Yield Financial Results That You Desire

"Both poverty and riches are the offspring of thought."
— NAPOLEON HILL

"Many folks think they aren't good at earning money, when what they don't know is how to use it."
— FRANK A. CLARK

"Money does not dictate your lifestyle, it's what you do to get it and how you manage your finances that determines your lifestyle."
— WAYNE CHIRISA

A Roadmap to Financial Success

Congratulations for making it this far. You have been on a long journey following the CLEAR WAY process to finding professional success. In this final chapter, I will invite you to look deeper into your relationship with money and identify any blind spots around money that may have been holding you back both during the process of choosing the line of work and with moving forward.

I have picked the tools that have been the most effective for my clients. First, I will discuss the importance of being able to speak about money in a comfortable neutral way. Then I will invite you to go deeper and identify the importance of differentiating between net worth and self-worth, especially as you begin communicating to potential employers, clients, or business partners/funds providers. You will then have an opportunity to look at your own money flow and identify the key opportunities for healing and growth. Finally, I will introduce the top tools and practices that my clients have effectively used to cultivate and nurture a healthy relationship with money to assist you in moving forward with your career.

Talk about Money Effectively

The first roadblock that most clients that I have worked with hit is the discomfort and unwillingness or inability to talk about money neutrally. Most of them have grown up in an environment where talking about money has not been healthy. Some households never discuss money and consider asking someone how much they make or caring about money as shameful and dirty and greedy. Others talk about money all the time but in a way that is always charged up with "it is never enough." My family didn't talk about money unless we were out of it. Of course there are always exceptions to the rules, but most clients who come through the door of my practice have challenges even thinking and speaking about money without getting very emotional. I am being very transparent and my professional career began in the area of finance at a large investment bank, so you would think I would be trained to talk about money in a healthy way. However, when it came down to personal finances, I remember my partner and I took five years before we finally began discussing our earnings and merging some of our finances. And there is nothing wrong with that. But if you are similar to me and didn't have an opportunity to learn how to talk about money in a positive way in your childhood, you will need to learn in some other way. To begin working with clients on the money area, I often first invite the client to share how often they think or talk about money with their loved ones and under what circumstances. How comfortable are they to talk about money to negotiate a salary or a business package?

In my coaching practice, the conversation around money comes up early. If a prospective client makes it to a stage where I choose to propose working together, we begin discussing the coaching fees. This is one of my most favorite parts, because in my experience, this is where the uncovered, unfiltered beliefs around money that the prospective client may have been hiding from herself will come out. And then we can get to the deep work of clearing those. I have seen incredible level of healing take place, simply from the client's willingness to talk honestly about money for an hour.

So step number one in this process is to be willing to talk to others about money. Then, of course, you want to watch the types of emotions that come up as you do. When I ask clients who are in the interview process about how comfortable they are to negotiate their salary or other forms of compensation, most get a bit emotional. This is all a part of learning how to talk about money in a neutral way. The key is to begin identifying and dis-identifying from the beliefs or interpretations that we have placed on money and the money conversations. It may sound simple, but it is often deep and uncomfortable work for many people, which is also incredibly powerful and effective. One of the things that I look for at this stage is the prospective client's willingness and ability to talk about money and their awareness of their own money situation. And I am also looking for what kind of beliefs and interpretations the clients share about money and what kind of feelings may be present. Once we have more awareness, we can go deeper into working with each one.

In my coaching groups we often do an exercise where the clients give themselves a written permission to talk about money (in a way that feels safe) and to learn, grow and to receive support on this journey. In my experience, most clients have expectations that they should know how to manage money when most of them have never had any positive role models to train them to do so; and most of the messages from the culture that they have received would be labeled "unhealthy."

An addition, a lot of clients come in with strong judgments about money or feeling that it is not OK to be focusing on it. I noticed that clients in my coaching groups typically fall into two buckets – the first bucket focuses on money as the top priority and the second bucket completely refuses to give it attention except in emergencies. In either case, clients often share how talking about money brings up feelings of stress and pressure.

If nothing else, one takeaway that I would love to leave you with is an invitation to develop a skill for discussing money in a neutral way, like you would discuss weather or your other skills. It will be imperative for negotiating compensation or fundraising for your business – we all need to be able to speak about money in a confident, neutral way. Clients who really struggle with this step find it helpful to begin to practice by engaging in conversations with close friends or making new friends who are willing and comfortable to talk about money in a positive way.

Net Worth Versus Self-Worth Versus Value of Service

The next piece that I often bring forward early on is busting a very common misunderstanding. I noticed that the overwhelming majority of clients who come in who want to focus on making more money confuse net worth with self-worth. And they also typically tangle the self-worth and the value of their service. And these entanglements create a very dangerous dynamic that puts a client in a very weak position for any money-related conversations and dramatically damages their ability to bring money into the lives. So let's take this one step at a time.

Net worth versus Self-Worth. Net worth is basically my assets (cash, savings, investments, or other items that I own and could sell, like my house and my car) less my liabilities (what I owe to others, such as student loans, car loan, house mortgage, any outstanding credit card balances, borrowing money from a friend or a family member). The balance is my "net worth." It could be positive or it could be negative. Most people have a lot of emotion attached to this number because they make an interpretation that their net worth is directly linked to their own value, their self-worth. So when net worth goes up, they feel good and when it goes down, they feel terrible and worthless. Most clients who come in have a version of this entanglement and our culture certainly promotes it. I have observed this entanglement creates such a wobbly foundation for our self-worth that it becomes very challenging to actually create a different situation, as the self-worth becomes too variable on external factors. And even when our net worth is very high, it often creates a situation of increased fear and anxiety of needing to keep it high so that the self-worth does not get affected.

If you suspect that you may have been mixing up your self-worth and your net worth, here is what I offer to my clients who want to work on separating the two. This is not easy to do, but it could be as simple as your willingness to change the interpretation that you place on your net worth. For example, instead of one interpretation, such as that your high net worth tells you that you are finally good enough and worthy of love, abundance, and appreciation, you can choose to interpret that your net worth shows you how well you manage your time, skills, and money, and it has nothing to do with your inherent value or your self-worth.

The truth that I want to offer you – and I offer this to every client and it may sound like a bold statement – is that your inherent value, your worth, is priceless. Inherently priceless. Period. There is nothing that you need to do to prove that or that you can do to change that. If you are raising eyebrows reading the above statement, I invite you to think of the last time you were around a baby. Imagine looking into that baby's eyes and holding its little fingers. What was the value of that baby? Did the value of that baby depend on its skills and talents? Did the value of that baby depend on how much money he or she was going to make in the future? Was the value of the baby higher or lower than the value of another baby? Of course not! Each baby is inherently priceless and is adored unconditionally.

I am here to remind you that you are that priceless child only in a grown body. The inherent value of a human does not change. You are not depreciating like a car as soon as you are born. And yet, most of my clients who share on this subject admit that they think of themselves and their self-worth in the self-depreciating way. So whatever work you can do to keep cultivating a healthy relationship with your self-worth as being independent of what you do and how much you have in your bank, the more freedom you will experience to actually create more money (if that is something that you choose to create). I know I am making strong statements here, and I will stand by them fully. I invite you to test them out for you. It has worked only 100 percent of the time with the clients that I have worked with!

Another entanglement in this category that I see often is a misidentification of the value of service and self-worth. As I have mentioned above, your inherent value is priceless. However, your service does have a value. So by separating the two, you can actually work on increasing the value of your service with a clear head without losing your foundation of your inherent self-worth and value.

I hope you are beginning to see the path that I invite you to follow here. The key takeaway from this section is that your inherent value, your foundation, is priceless. You are priceless and there is nothing we can or need to do to change that. Standing strong in this knowing, you then have freedom to discuss, analyze, and increase the value of your services so that you can generate the money that you choose. Generating and keeping more money becomes a lot more fun and more consistent too because your foundation of self-worth is solid.

Identify Blind Spots about Money

As we begin identifying the key entanglements around money clients share the messages around money that they have inherited from their families. In many ways, I see clients walking in with many different types of "inherence," their genes, talents, abilities, life experiences, habits, and their own unique way of how they think and relate with money. Unless a client had been fortunate to grow up in a household that was very prosperous and had a healthy relationship with money, most of them could greatly benefit from deeper work around identifying and clearing any limiting beliefs and misinterpretations around money. One exercise that I often give to my clients is to take some time and complete simple sentences, such as the following:

Money is _____.

I learned from my mother that money is _____.

I learned from my father that money is _____.

I wish money was _____.

Money is always _____.

Money is never _____.

It is very revealing to begin to pay attention and challenge the core beliefs around money that you may have been using as programs for your mind and for creating your lives.

See if you identify yourself with any of these that I hear often:

- Money or wanting money is bad and dirty.
- Money doesn't grow on trees.
- I have to sell my soul to make more money.
- People who focus on money are evil.
- Money comes from a job/employer.

- Starting a business is not a real job; you need to be realistic and have a steady paycheck.
- You have to people please to make money.
- You don't have to like your job as long as you have a paycheck.
- Men make more money than women.
- Men don't like or are threatened by women who make more money than them.

Did you identify with any of these? What are some of the ones that came up for you? I invite you to take a look at your own list and reflect on how well your own money beliefs are working for you. If not so well, would you be willing to test out a different filtering system for thinking about money?

This is when clients often identify some big limitations, and it pays (literally) to slow down and do some inner work on clearing the misinterpretations with more updated beliefs.

A great exercise if you want to go bold is to make some new friends with people who have a healthy relationship with money and begin to actively pay attention to how they talk about money. Most likely you will notice a big difference right away, and it may be easier to spot some of the key blind spots that you have. Or I also often recommend to clients to begin to journal and reflect on how their spouse, significant loved ones, and they themselves talk about money. This step is very important for working through and replacing the old programs. What are the core themes? What is the general attitude towards money? You will often notice similar patterns very quickly.

Money Flow: Balancing Inflows and Outflows

As the client gets deeper into the inner work around rewiring any limiting patterns and thinking programs they may have around money, we often begin to look at the way that money flows in and out of their lives to see where the key problems are.

Some clients struggle with bringing more income. Most clients consider this to be their primary concern. However, in my experience, in addition to analyzing the inflows, it is equally as important to see how the clients spend/allocate the money that comes in. I found it most effective to work on both the inflow of money, as well as developing skills and practices that support a client with intentional and healthy spending and investing. Discussing best practices for spending and investing is outside of the scope of this book; however, it could be supportive even at the early stages of the interview or business building process to do a basic estimate of how much money you spend per month to get a sense of your financial needs. If you have never done that, I would take the financial statements for the last three months and evaluate your most common expenses and average spending. You can choose to do a lot more work on intentionally allocating and trimming those, but at the very least, you want to have a good sense of how much money you want to generate to support your existing expenses as you lean into your new career.

Increase Earnings: Compensation Formula

Earning is a part of the process of choosing what to do and actually moving forward. After working with many clients and continually revising my own process, I have created a basic formula for money coming in.

Let me explain.

Value of service is, of course, highly variable, based on who the client is, the actual product or service that you are selling, and, if you are working for a company, your position and how well it is utilizing your skills and talents. So this piece has a lot to do with also aligning your service with the client/employer who will be receiving the full value of it.

If you are a business owner and you want to make more money, you can reflect on the question, "How can I increase the value of service that I provide?" This is a much more effective and idea-generating question instead of getting caught up in a fearful thought pattern that I hear often – "I need to pay rent and I need money! What if this client/customer drops out, what will I do?"

If you are working for an employer, in addition to evaluating how to increase value that you provide with your skills and talents, you also want to reflect on if the service that you provide is the right fit for your employer.

The second piece of the formula is the number of people you serve. As a business owner, it is especially powerful to think about this one – "How can I increase the number of people that I serve? Is it time to scale?" As an employee, it may not be as obvious, but there is a corresponding link as well, depending on the line of work that you are in.

And finally, the least defined, but a very important variable is your openness to receive. This one is an interesting one and the least tangible. Lack of openness to receive can show up in many harmful ways. For example, I remember working with this amazing client, a coach, very talented, with powerful and big ideas, but she kept offering her services for free because she had a lot of inner blocks around recognizing the value of her service (notice this is different from the actual value of her service), and she had misinterpretations that charging for her service was greedy. She didn't feel that her services were as valuable as her clients saw them. In other words, she was not open to receive. As soon as we did work around changing her relationship with receiving, revenue began to flow in.

Openness to receive can also look like being willing to negotiate and talk about salary options and other compensation topics during the negotiation process. Openness to receive also looks like having a clean and organized way to process payments for your business. In summary, openness to receive clears up anything that is in the way of you actually receiving compensation for your services.

Given the space limitations of the book format, I chose to focus on the key areas around money that I have found to be the most relevant to a successful transition into a new career. That said, I want to share some additional tools to support you with cultivating a healthy relationship with money once you have shifted into your dream career to ensure success going forward.

Hiring Money to Work for You

I found that money is similar to any other partner that you may have in your life: building a healthy relationship can take some love, attention, and nurturing, but it will be incredibly rewarding in the long run. I like to think of approaching money as an employee and "hiring money to work for you." There are so many ways do this, and having a clear intention is the first step.

One exercise that I often offer my clients is to write an honest letter to money, sharing their feelings, gratitude, fears, or anything that might be present. First, most people get very surprised by the idea, but then it is always incredibly revealing. I have had clients write love letters to money, and I have had clients write letters of accusation (Money where have you been all my life?). I also have had clients ask money for business advice. I thought it was brilliant!

And then the next step in this exercise is to have money "write you a letter." It may sound odd at the beginning, but it is as simple as sitting down with a pen and paper and setting an intention to allow money to write "through" you. And then just write whatever comes up. You cannot do this wrong! This is when the relationship typically goes deeper and I always love hearing business ideas that money would "share." I once had a client create her entire business plan for the year after writing these two letters. She got so many ideas from writing the "response letter" that she completely turned her business upside down!

The intention here is to begin to see money as an important partner in your life, who is here to serve and support you. It is not a master, but it is not an unpaid intern either. Just like with any other relationship that we care about, in my experience, it pays to spend some time and energy to nurture a loving and healthy relationship with money. It will serve you for the rest of your life!

One other exercise for those who are deeply committed is to create a vision for their ideal relationship with money. Clients have a lot of fun with this one; many bring pictures, write love wishes, and include affirmations, mantras, and poems. I had one client who created a video with uplifting music as a background, and she watched it regularly. The key is to create some space in your life for money to be a part of it, so that you can all enjoy each other. How fun would that be?

Chapter Highlights

- Give yourself permission to talk about money and to learn, grow, and receive support on this journey.
- Most people tend to have expectations that they should know how to manage money when most have never had any positive role models to train them to do so.
- Being able to speak about money in a neutral way is pivotal to salary negotiations and fundraising for a business.
- Most clients that I have worked with have inherited "scarcity" and limited types of beliefs and interpretations about money, and it has been truly life changing to identify and update those beliefs.

- To maximize effectiveness I invite you to focus on streamlining both the inflows and the outflows of money.
- Money Inflow Formula:

$$\text{Income} = \text{Value of Service} \times \text{\# of People that You Serve} \times \text{Openness to Receive Money}$$

- Cultivating a healthy relationship with money is key and a fun way to guarantee a fun life with money as a loyal partner and devoted employee that cooperates with you and supports you every step of the way!

Suggested Next Steps and Exercises

- Reflect on the key messages about money from your parents, significant others, and your culture and then question how they are serving you. Would you like to update any of these? If yes, dive in and use the tools for rewriting your thinking programs to do so.
- Have a conversation about money with someone you trust (with their permission) in a way that is positive and curious.
- Build in "dates with money" into your calendar on a regular basis, where you spend time with money, either by going to your bank accounts, paying bills, learning about investing, creating ways to bring more money in, and so on. The key is to approach it with love and appreciation as you would with taking your loved one on a date!

- Test out the exercise: Write a letter to money and let money write back. Ask for specific questions regarding money.
- Create a vision for the Ideal Relationship with Money. Example: How much money do I want to make? What do I hope to experience once I have the money? What do I want money for? How do I want to show up for the money that comes into my life? How do I want to be treated by money? And how do I promise to treat money? How would you like money to support you with your heartfelt desire, your Sacred YES vision? What would you like money to do for you? What would you be willing to do in return?

Chapter 11:

Get Ready for the Next Steps

"It's a funny thing about life: if you refuse to accept anything but the best, you very often get it."
— W. Somerset Maugham

Celebrate Your CLEAR WAY Journey: Recap

I acknowledge you for taking this journey with me. I wrote this book in hopes to share the key tools that I have found most effective with the clients in my practice. Each one of them came in overwhelmed with his or her talents and gifts, struggling to choose what to do. And each was able to find both his or her niche and a more rich, meaningful, and full life.

I want to recap the key principles with you, as we are parting ways.

C: Cultivate a State Where Clarity Is Possible

In Chapter 3, I discussed clarity as a natural state of awareness and how, deep down, you already know what you want to do and how it is a matter of knowing what that is. You learned tools for developing the mastery of the art of listening for inner wisdom, what you need to know as you make all choices and especially as you begin to choose your niche.

L: Learn How to Dream Effectively

In Chapter 4, you worked on identifying and removing blind spots around putting limits on your dreams and the importance of taking the lid off what you think is possible so that you can choose what is truly in alignment with what you want so that you can create long-lasting success.

E: Enlist a Vision That Is a Sacred Yes

In Chapter 5, I laid out tools and practices for creating a vision that is a Sacred Yes and the importance of creating a vision that fits into a life that you want. I also discussed the difference between clarity of the entire vision and clarity of next steps and the power to become very effective and to maximize momentum.

A: Access Your Personal Success Formula

In Chapter 6, I explained how you can discover your unique success formula, including what moves you to action and your way of making choices.

R: Receive Maximum Return on Your Energy Investments

In Chapter 7, you learned how to work with your natural flow of energy as you begin to take action and learn how to maximize the effectiveness of your energy investments.

W: Wire Resistance to Work for You

In Chapter 8, you got clarity on how exactly resistance shows up in your life and how to most effectively work with it and use it to accelerate your progress as you begin to take action.

A: Align Thoughts and Emotions for Success

In Chapter 9, I shared tools for working with feelings and thoughts that are not constructive to your vision to support yourself in moving forward.

Y: Yield Financial Results That You Desire

In Chapter 10, you identified your key blind spots around the flow of money and began to work on developing a healthy relationship with money.

* * *

My intention for writing this book was to support you in becoming aware of the blind spots that you have been operating with in regard to choosing your profession. I want you to know that you can choose what to do and begin to take action that is in deep resonance with all parts of you.

The world needs the special light that only you can provide.

As Marianne Williamson said, "Our greatest fear is not that we are inadequate, it is that we are powerful beyond measure. ... Who are we not to be?"

Chapter 12:

Tips for the Journey Ahead

"Life is not a solo act. It's a huge collaboration, and we all need to assemble around us the people who care about us and support us in times of strife."
— TIM GUNN

Create a Support Container for Your Dream

When Roxanne first came in, she confessed that she had been attempting to get clarity and move forward for several years. In many ways, quitting her job was a symbol of hope that in this big gesture she would get instant clarity of what exactly she wanted to do and how she wanted to proceed. She was confused and disappointed that for some reason after the adrenaline and excitement of quitting wore off, she felt even more confused and mildly depressed. She felt like she should have all the answers; after all, she had two graduate degrees. Everyone was expecting her to have the answers, and Roxanne felt a lot of shame for not being able to figure it out.

I see this a lot in other clients, and I certainly have experienced this myself too. I believe our culture trains us to take pride in figuring things out on our own, and we especially expect the educated professionals to be able to easily choose what to do on their own. However, the people who are very successful have intentionally worked in all the areas of choosing and making commitments that we had covered in the book; and everyone, including me, has received a lot of support. So the first obstacle that I see that many people who come into my practice need to overcome is letting go of the dangerous idea that they need to figure things out on their own, that they can't trust anyone else to support them unless they give up completely. I have seen more lives being broken, money wasted, relationships estranged, and dreams killed by pride from what Robert Holden calls "dysfunctional independence." We then wonder why we feel so lonely and why we feel stuck. So the first step is to be willing to receive support.

Receive the RIGHT Support

Then there comes the next step. You want to make sure that you received the right support and that it comes in a way that is empowering for you to move forward and grow instead of feeling like you need to be "rescued."

In my observation, most clients who come into my practice searching for clarity claim that they have attempted to receive assistance and support from other places. When I get curious about what kind of support they have solicited, I typically hear about various personality and skills/talents assessments. These types of support are great and can be very helpful and I have certainly used assessments at various stages of my own life and with the clients. However, what I listen for is how the client has been using the results of the tests. Here is what I see: A person is looking for answers and hoping that a multiple-choice test will basically tell him or her what to do. This is so limiting and never fulfilling because we are so unique and no test can ever truly give us an answer or choose our path for us. But I see how there is a small part in most of us that is hoping to be rescued by a very smart test. Tests are great, and in my experience, it is all about how we use the results, but they can never substitute the deeper work that is required to truly begin to make choices that are aligned and centered in your heart.

Another version of the rescue fantasy that I see is clients hoping that a career counselor or a mentor or even a psychic (yep, I have heard that one on multiple occasions) will have a better answer for them than they do. If you can relate, notice how in this situation you are outsourcing your own wisdom and self-reliance and trust in yourself to make choices to someone else. In my experience, even with the best advice, this approach can take you only so far, because even if you get some help in getting an idea for which direction to move into, you still need to learn how to make decisions and how to choose for you so that you can proceed successfully. And unless that work is done, you are most likely to find yourself stuck very quickly again and will either stay stuck or will need continual validation to keep moving forward. It is a lot more effective to learn how to make choices once and for all, so that your move into action can be smooth, long lasting, and effective.

With regard to making choices, as we began working together, Roxanne learned very quickly that she had been trying to navigate and drive with her metaphorical windshield completely fogged up. No wonder she kept getting stuck and felt like she was getting nowhere. In my experience, we all have blind spots in our thinking, and by definition, it is very hard to see what they are, hence why the right level of support can be so powerful. And yet, most of us are expecting to solve the problem with the same type of thinking that created it in the first place. This Einstein quote comes to mind, "It is the definition of insanity to keep taking the same action and expect a different result." I like to paraphrase it and apply it to thinking. In my experience unless we do intentional work on recognizing and reprogramming our thinking, we tend to spin our wheels.

Dissolve the Most Common Blind Spot

The most common blind spot that I see in the clients that I work with is a version of lack of trust, in themselves, others, and the world at large.

These are some examples that I have seen most often:

- I don't trust my decisions about money or work or anything
- I cannot be consistent with anything
- I am untrustworthy – I cannot trust myself to follow through on my dream
- I can never change
- I am different from all the other people who have found work that they love. I have different talents or background or challenges – whatever worked for others will never work for me
- I just don't know how to choose, it is just who I am
- I am allergic to commitment
- I will never be able to make enough money doing what I love so I won't even bother trying
- I cannot trust anyone else, as nobody really cares

These doubts can seem incredibly convincing. Here is what I noticed: All of these doubts are proven to be true for the people who are thinking this and they are not true for the people who don't.

I discussed in depth limiting beliefs and filters. My invitation is to evaluate if the program that you are running in your head will produce the result that you desire. So if you are running "I can never change" program, you will continue to subconsciously resist change and find ways to prove to yourself that you "cannot change." That is why without support and deep inner reflection it can take so long to get out of the experience of being stuck.

Roxanne is not the only one who came with a problem of needing to choose what to do. I had another client, Allison, who came in with a steady job that paid over six figures, and she was satisfied with many aspects of her job, except that she felt antsy, restless to start her business, and she felt like she had been waiting for her life to begin. At thirty-seven, she was in mental agony, had developed anxiety, and had a hard time sleeping. When she came in, she confessed that for a while she convinced herself that she didn't have a problem with her career, because she had a prestigious job that paid her bills and 401K contributions with money left over for vacations and yoga retreats, but she felt so stuck and unhappy. She spent two years in therapy, working with multiple people, hoping to solve the problem. She has learned a lot about herself, but she finally allowed herself to admit that the voice that was pushing her to leave was the voice of her heart. So when she showed up, she was so uncomfortable already that she was committed and ready for action.

During our first conversation Allison admitted that she was paralyzed with the fear of leaving her job too soon and failing financially in her business, so she wanted to prepare for her transition very carefully. We focused on that and about six months later Allison had a plan in place for how she would be navigating her transition out of the old career and into the new business. She felt alive and in action, excited and ready to give the notice to her boss and to step into the next phase of her professional life.

I want to share one other story – Tom. He came in with student loans and credit card debt requesting support with preparing him to get a lucrative job in finance or similar. It would have been fine, but Tom's motivation was to get a job in finance with the sole purpose of making money, even though his entire body/mind/emotions were not on board, so he struggled getting interviews. I am all for smart financial planning, and I don't think that there is anything wrong with investing time in generating and saving cash or fundraising actively so that you later can focus on a more creative part of a business. However, in my experience, it makes all the difference if you do the work up-front to get clarity on what is the Sacred YES and do not wait to choose what to do.

What I offered Tom is to shift his aim slightly. What if it is not an either/or scenario? What if he could begin shifting into doing the work that he loved while also still learning how to take care of finances? What if he could increase his standards instead of "settling" for a job he wasn't enthusiastic about? As we explored together, Tom had an "aha" moment and completely revamped his strategy for the job search. The shift quickly led to different types of interviews and new exciting job opportunities that he previously would have simply not been aware of.

I remember hearing Warren Buffett sharing a funny quote on the subject of "saving doing the work that you love for later years is like saving having sex for old age."

My invitation for you is to stop waiting, connect to your Sacred YES vision and begin taking action steps as soon as you can. Your vision is waiting for you!

Acknowledgments

It was a warm afternoon in June before my senior year in high school. I was enjoying the pleasant breeze while sitting on the balcony in our post-Soviet apartment in Dzerzhinsk, Russia. I just finished reading my first self-help book on the power of setting goals and life visions by a very enthusiastic American author, Tony Robbins. Inspired by the author and his stories, I took out a weathered notebook with a hard blue cover, found a blank page and scribbled my top ten life goals.

Goal number one was to write and publish a book.

Over the years I have created many life visions and writing a book has always stayed as one of my top life goals.

It is now twenty years later and I am sitting at my favorite desk in my home in Santa Monica, typing up this page with my book launching in a couple of weeks. With a heart full of gratitude I am reflecting on how many people had touched my life to make this book possible. Some knew how much they had impacted me and some may never know.

There is no way I can ever thank everyone.

First of all, to my coach Angela and her team at the Author Incubator. I can confidently say that without your support I would not be an author today. Thank you for your guidance, patience, and loving support to make this book a reality.

To my mom, dad and sister Svetlana, who have believed in me since I was very young and who have been so understanding and loving with my process of writing this book.

To James who has inspired me to grow in ways I had never expected and who has helped me stay centered and focused during the editing and publishing stage of this book's journey. You inspire me every day and I am deeply grateful for your love and support.

To my dear friends Mandy, Sandy, Patricia, Arielle, Joanna, Joanne, Courtney, Anthony, Ashley, Andrew, David, Guru Amrit Hari and many more who have continuously showed up for me and held the vision for the book's successful completion high. Your friendship is deeply meaningful to me.

To the participants of the beta *Awaken Your Career* program who have trusted me and signed up for the program before I have published the book and before I have created all the lesson plans. Your stories, questions and feedback made this book and the program so much richer. Each one of you has a place in my heart.

To Ron and Mary Hulnick, who have been my teachers for the past seven years. I can confidently say that this book would not have been written without all the powerful experiences that I have had at the University of Santa Monica and without all the tools and practices that I have learned from you.

To Amber Krzys, who was my coach right before I wrote the book. Working with you have inspired me to play a much bigger game of service. Your presence and loving support during the last year have been instrumental and taught me the power of holding a vision for someone else and the beauty of transforming obstacles into the stepping stones.

To all my classmates and the larger community at the University of Santa Monica. Your love and support in the moments of struggle and self-doubt have elevated me to a place where I could keep going forward in an expansive state.

To everyone at Coachmasters, my Toastmasters club. Thank you for providing a safe and fun space for me to share personal stories and discover my voice as a speaker and a coach, which later translated into finding my voice as a writer for this book.

To the team at Training The Street, Inc. Your mentorship and nurturance for almost ten years have been instrumental in my growth as a teacher, a businesswoman and a coach. And Thank you for the opportunity to have a taste of professional writing when trusting me with being a contributing writer for the self-study materials. I am deeply grateful for all of it.

I would also like to acknowledge the Morgan James Publishing Team: David Hancock, CEO & Founder; my Author Relations Manager, Tiffany Gibson; and special thanks to Jim Howard, Bethany Marshall, and Nickcole Watkins.

I am so full of love and gratitude as I am reflecting on how many people have been a part of my journey!

My intention is to keep serving and keep sharing everything that I have learned and received from you with others as best as I can.

In Loving Gratitude,
Valentina

About the Author

Valentina Savelyeva is a professional certified success coach, author, and motivational speaker. She specializes in working with professionals and business owners from all over the world to take the next step in their careers. Before opening her international coaching practice in Los Angeles, Valentina spent a  decade leading financial workshops and training programs as one of the top instructors at a leading Wall Street–based company training the next generation of financial professionals. Valentina delivered highly sought-out programs to raving reviews at top business schools and financial and consulting firms all over the United States and Europe, averaging ninety to one hundred lectures a year for over six years. Her corporate and academic clients included over thirty institutions such as Harvard Business School, USC Marshall School of Business, UCLA Anderson

School of Management, Wharton School of the University of Pennsylvania, Credit Suisse, UBS, Citigroup, Wells Fargo, Deloitte, Boston Consulting Group, and many more.

Valentina has been an avid student in the self-development field for twenty years. She has had the privilege of training with some of the most accomplished coaches in the industry, including Steve Chandler (*Time Warrior, Crazy Good*), Robert Holden (*Authentic Success, Lovability*), Ron and Mary Hulnick (*Loyalty to Your Soul*), Steven McGhee (*Get Real*), and Carolyn Freyer-Jones, among many others. She holds an MA in spiritual psychology from the University of Santa Monica and BS in business administration from Haas School of Business at UC Berkeley.

Valentina is excited to take her skills as a trainer, facilitator, and coach from MBA auditoriums and corporate boardrooms into the public world with her custom *Awaken Your Career* program teaching the CLEAR WAY Framework, individual coaching programs, seminars, books, and speaking engagements.

Valentina currently resides in Santa Monica, California. She loves spending time with her loved ones, laughing and being silly, hiking in the mountains, enjoying the ocean, reading, meditating, dancing, painting, and appreciating life as fully as she can.

For more information about Valentina, you can find her on:

Website: clearwaycoach.com
Email: valentina@clearwaycoach.com
LinkedIn: linkedin.com/in/vsavelyeva/

Thank You

Thank you for reading *Get Clear on Your Career*!

This isn't the end, but rather the beginning of an exciting journey as you choose the work that you LOVE! I sincerely hope this book has provided you with some ideas for how to get clear on what you want to do and some practical tools for moving forward.

If you haven't done so yet, I invite you to watch the supplemental master class on How to *Handle Fear Effectively*. You can download it here: clearwaycoach.com/free

Enjoy!

Valentina
clearwaycoach.com
valentina@clearwaycoach.com